THE WINES OF CHILE

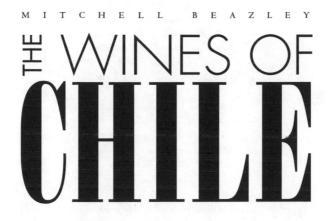

MITCHELL BEAZLEY

THE WINES OF CHILE

JAN READ

FOREWORD BY HUGH JOHNSON

First published in Great Britain in 1994 by
Mitchell Beazley
an imprint of
Reed Consumer Books Limited
Michelin House, 81 Fulham Road
London SW3 6RB
and Auckland, Melbourne, Singapore and Toronto

© 1994 Reed International Books Limited

Text copyright © Jan Read, 1994
Maps © Reed International Books Limited, 1994

ISBN 1 85732 330 0

Although all reasonable care has been taken in the
preparation of this book, neither the author nor the
publishers can accept liability for any consequences
arising from the information contained herein, or
from the use thereof.

A CIP catalogue record for this book is available
from the British Library

Executive Editor: Anne Ryland
Art Director: Jacqui Small
Editor: Anthea Snow
Art Editor: Paul Tilby
Index: Ann Barrett
Map artwork: Bob Reed
Production: Michelle Thomas

Printed and bound in Hong Kong
Typeset in Linotype Centaur/Monotype Bembo

CONTENTS

ACKNOWLEDGEMENTS

My thanks must first go to the Asociación de Exportadores y Embotalledores de Vinos AG for inviting my wife and myself to Chile to undertake the research for this book. Between them, Don Pablo Hurtado of the Asociación in Santiago and Wines of Chile in London worked out a complicated schedule for visits to some 30 wineries. I am also most grateful to Doña Pilar Yrarrazaval Morande and Doña Sylvia Cava of the Dirección General de Relaciones Economicas Internacionales (PROCHILE) for making further arrangements in Chile. Apart from these official bodies and their staff, Don Miguel Torres of Vinícola Miguel Torres SA and Mr Douglas Murray of Discover Wine SA were of major assistance in making possible and planning the visit. The winemakers who welcomed us to their bodegas are too numerous to thank individually, but without their help and lively interest it would, of course, have been impossible to write the book. Others whom we were unable to visit have been generous in despatching their wines to us for tasting.

I am indebted to Professor Alejandro Hernández, Dean of the Faculty of Oenology at the Universidad Católica de Chile, and to Mr Douglas Murray for allowing me to quote from the paper they presented to the OIV Convention in San Francisco in August 1993, and to Don Rodrigo Alvarado Moore for the short extract reproduced from the Orbis *Enciclopédia del Vino*.

Doña Josette Grand kindly contributed two of her delicious recipes to the chapter on Chilean cooking, and Doña María Ignacia Echenique also helped with that section. Eight recipes have been adapted from *Chile, Una Cocina*, an excellent booklet in Spanish and English, which is recommended.

And not for the first time special thanks go to my wife, Maite Manjón, for the chapter on Chilean food and for acting as interpreter, organizer and taster.

FOREWORD
by HUGH JOHNSON

As we entered the last decade of the 20th century, Chile slid with a satisfying click into its preordained place in the world of wine.

Its arrival had been long and frustratingly delayed. It has been an open secret for many years that Chile grows wonderful grapes with disdainful ease. Its perfect climate – or rather choice of climates – seems to have thermostats set precisely where vines want them to be. Its soils are deep and fertile. The Andes provide unfailing water for irrigation – and have successfully kept out phylloxera. Vines (mainly from Bordeaux) have been flourishing here for 150 years. 'What are they waiting for?' is the question you are bound to ask.

Jan Read and I asked it when we visited Chile together ten years ago. There we found an inward-looking wine industry. Ten years before that, I had seen the chaos caused by an attempt at communism which sent landowners into exile. The right-wing years that followed were not conducive to rapid progress. Jan and I found winemakers either complacent with out-of-date methods and materials or frustrated because they could not afford to change them. We saw perfect grapes too often turned into faulty wine. We wrote a book together, dispassionately describing the state of affairs. It is tempting to quote Molière: '*Nous avons changé tout cela*' – but it is too pat. Not we, but they, have changed all that, with a determined drive to re-equip and reorientate that has given the world what may well amount to a second California within a few brief years.

Chile has found its destiny. It is only right that the writer and oenologist who more than anyone spurred it on should report and celebrate Chile's emergence as one of the world's great wine-lands, ready for the 21st century. Jan Read, long steeped in the history, science and culture of wine in the Spanish world, is uniquely able to put this great new resource into perspective for us.

INTRODUCTION

Since I first went to Chile in 1984 with Hugh Johnson to write a book about the wines, sweeping changes have occurred in the wine industry there. Modern technology in the shape of controlled fermentation in stainless steel and maturation in small oak barrels of American and French oak, the training of Chilean oenologists in California, France, Australia and New Zealand, and the emergence of small 'boutique' wineries have all contributed to great improvements in the quality of the wines. This is particularly so in the case of the varietal white wines; many of the Chilean Cabernet Sauvignons were already very good. The gauge of this is that since 1984 exports of bottled wine have increased by 1,000 percent.

Chilean wine is now taking its place beside other fine growths from the New World. It is however produced by a small number of concerns, albeit the biggest are large by world standards. I have tried to cover all those of note in an A–Z section describing the individual wineries and their wines, and including detailed tasting notes of the whole range of wines made by each.

Since little is known abroad about Chilean wine production, there are also comprehensive chapters on subjects such as: the fascinating history of winemaking in Chile; vines, vineyards and winemaking; pisco, the Moscatel-based brandy; and the cooking, an intriguing blend of Indian, Spanish and French.

Anyone who travels halfway across the world, whether professionally involved in wine or simply an enthusiast, will want to see more of Chile than its wineries. When I first went, I fell in love with the mountains, the flowers and trees, the sunshine and limpid atmosphere, and the friendliness of the people. I have therefore begun the book by trying to give an impression of the country which I hope may interest travellers, armchair or otherwise, together with some practical notes for those who sit out the 8,000 air miles.

THE FAR COUNTRY

After writing a biography of Lord Cochrane, that Scots seaman extraordinary who played a key role in the struggle for Chilean independence, I had always wanted to visit the country. The chance came when I was asked to write a book on Chilean wines, and I was not disappointed with what I found. I suppose that every visitor's idea of Chile and Peru is of the 'snow-capped Andes', but Chile turned out to be a most varied and surprising country, so like and yet so unlike Spain.

The Andes *are*, of course, ever-present. In a country 4,200 kilometres (some 3,000 miles) long, but never more than about 180 kilometres (110 miles) wide, they either tower above you, as in the capital, Santiago, or lie along the horizon in a misty blue line. Down the whole length of the country, between the Andes and the coastal hills with the Pacific beyond there runs a valley depression, sometimes broken by mountain spurs. The contrasts in climate and scenery over this great length are extreme. The first 1,250 kilometres (780 miles) from the Peruvian frontier in the north (corresponding to Regions I and II of the 13 into which the country is divided) comprise baked brown desert, the site of the famous nitrate deposits and copper mines. The next 600 kilometres (370 miles) are broken by great mountain massifs running down towards the sea, and fertile valleys – this is pisco country. The heartland of Chile, where most people live, is the Central Valley, extending from Regions V to VII, a Garden of Eden with a perfect Mediterranean climate, where vineyards and orchards abound. South of Concepción in

Regions IX and X lies a land of lakes, rivers and mountains, as wet as Scotland, and like Scotland a walkers' and fishers' paradise. Beyond that, from Puerto Montt to Cape Horn, stretch 1,600 kilometres (1,000 miles) of wild mountains, glaciers, fjords and islands, cold and stormy with torrential rain. If Chile were not so far, it might well be more popular with holiday-makers. It has all the right ingredients: hundreds of miles of unspoilt Pacific beaches; riding, fishing, canoeing and skiing; good, modestly priced wine, and over much of the country an almost perfect climate, with months of completely unbroken sunshine during summer (which corresponds to winter in Europe or North America). Around Santiago and in the Central Valley temperatures rise to about 33°C (91°F), but it is not humid or sticky, and temperatures fall at night thanks to the cold offshore Humboldt Current (which is also responsible for the excellent quality of the shellfish).

AIRLINES, RAILWAYS AND ROADS

From the UK it is possible to fly to Chile via Buenos Aires, Rio de Janeiro or Miami. Depending on the route and stopovers, flights take between 18 and 24 hours; from New York the flying time is about 18 hours. The flight across the Andes with its network of peaks, craters, snowfields, mountain tracks zig-zagging up to the first settlements and broad green valleys opening out onto the plains below, is simply unforgettable. Inside Chile, flying is the best way to travel if distances are large, as to Arica or La Serena in the north or Punta Arenas in Patagonia to the south. Apart from the national airline LAN-Chile and the privately owned and extremely comfortable Ladeco, various small airlines fly small planes in which the co-pilot will produce a bottle of whisky from beneath his seat and serve it en route.

For the railway buff, if not for the speed or comfort of the trains, Chile is most definitely recommended. Passenger services on the vertiginous Transandine Line to Buenos Aires have, alas, been suspended, as have most of the narrow-gauge lines north of Santiago which have reverted to the purpose for which they were built by the British, for transporting nitrate and copper ore. There are, however, trains from Valparaíso via Viña del Mar to Los

Andes along the Transandine metals; and even in the port of Coquimbo, near La Serena, visitors may be surprised to see the occasional unscheduled train enter an impressive and apparently deserted station via the streets before disappearing with a bevy of country folk in the direction of the Andes.

For practical purposes, the one viable line is the electrified trunk route from Santiago to Concepción, Valdivia and places south. From Santiago to Talca there are fast daytime trains serving the wine towns of the Central Valley – Buin, Rancagua, Curicó and the rest – and a comfortable long-distance night train equipped with German sleeping coaches of early 1900s vintage, with berths arranged lengthwise to smoothen the ride along the somewhat bumpy track.

The trains are increasingly less used, the main axis of communication being the Pan American Highway. This is a well-engineered road with long stretches of double carriageway, spanning Chile from the Peruvian border in the north to Puerto Montt in the south.

South of Santiago is the wine area of the Central Valley. It is bordered by motels, restaurants, nurseries displaying roses and fruit trees, stalls selling pottery, wickerwork and straw hats, and a succession of gleaming, modern fruit-packing plants. Because the country is so thin, it is never more than an hour's drive to the wineries lying either side of the highway.

SCENERY, ARCHITECTURE AND SIGHTSEEING

The vast deserts of northern Chile, the rocky Pacific coastline and stony mountainsides rising sheer into an azure sky, are scenery on a heroic scale, but what is particularly striking in the wine country of the Central Valley is the wealth of trees and flowers. The vineyards are often flanked with Lombardy poplars; one knowledgeable chauffeur explained that these mark the limits of individual properties (in this he was better informed than another driver, a city dweller from Santiago, who, gesturing towards a mountainside of cacti, told us that they were pines used for firewood in the winter!). Many of the trees, such as the weeping willows which line the watercourses and irrigation canals, the towering eucalypti, planted in groves along the roads and around the bodegas, and the fruit trees of the huge orchards, are not native to Chile. Almost anything thrives; as Vice-Admiral John Byron, grandfather of the famous Lord Byron, or 'Foul-weather Jack' as he was nicknamed by his sailors, once remarked: 'The soil of the country is so fertile, that the husbandmen have very little trouble; for they do but in a manner scratch up the ground, and without any kind of manure it yields an hundred fold.' Among the most remarkable collections of exotic trees are those in the parks of the Cousiño family at Macul on the outskirts of Santiago, and those at Lota near Concepción in the south. It is said that the cedars of Lebanon in the Macul park are among the finest in the world.

Roses grow everywhere in patios and gardens, and wild dog-roses run riot along the country roads. Every winery has its brilliantly coloured ornamental garden with purple bougainvillaea, pink and white oleander, blue plumbago and jacaranda, the exotic red trumpets of the copihue, and fiery pepper trees.

Not much Spanish architecture still exists. Most of the old buildings of the colonial period were destroyed by earthquakes, some of them severe, like those which wrecked Santiago in 1822, 1835, 1868 and 1875. In milder form they are an everyday occurrence. One day I was sitting with Sr Fernando Herrera in his office at Pisco Control in La Serena, when there was a dull thud and tremor. He broke off. The thud was repeated and the bottles in front of us shook. '*Un terremoto,*' he explained, and went on with what he was saying.

The occurrence of earthquakes explains why most of the older stone churches have been rebuilt with wooden steeples and wood is often used for the imposing, colonial-style country houses with their pillars and verandas. Most Chilean cities and towns have at their centre a Plaza de Armas, the old garrison parade ground, but these are Spanish in name alone and are flanked by modern buildings. In Santiago there are one or two magnificent 18th-century colonial buildings, such as the old mint, the Palacio de la Moneda, and the Casa Colorada, now the Museum of Santiago, but most of the large public buildings are in the style of the French Belle Epoque dating from the late 19th century, and there are now many modern high-rise office and apartment blocks.

Santiago – thanks to the dramatic backdrop of the Andes, the Mapocho River which runs through its centre, its many parks, and the residential areas with their tree-lined streets and vivid gardens – is an attractive city, and the fifth largest in South America with a population of 4,850,000. Of its many restaurants, particularly interesting to wine-lovers is the Enoteca halfway up the 840-metre (2,500-foot) Cerro San Cristobal, a spur of the Andes pushing its way into the heart of the city and now a vast metropolitan park. A handsome colonnaded building with interior patio and a lower floor devoted to a wine museum and tasting room, it mounts a permanent exhibition of Chilean wines with free tastings of the 'wine of the day'.

On the coast to the north of Santiago is Chile's largest seaport, Valparaíso, and just beyond it the favourite seaside resort of the Santiaguinos, Viña del Mar. There are no longer vineyards at Viña, although to the south lies the new and promising wine area of Casablanca, and it is Chile's second largest city with a population of approximately 300,000. Its Hotel Miramar is one of the country's best. To enter its huge dining room with palms in tubs, panoramic windows overlooking the sea and waiters in evening dress is to step straight into the 1930s. The coast north of Viña del Mar is very much built up, reminiscent of the Costa del Sol in Spain and definitely for the gregarious.

Valparaíso is a place of great character, climbing up the steep slopes of a crescent of hills facing the sea. Little of the old colonial city survives, a massive earthquake in 1906 having completed the devastations of pirates, fires and storms. The commercial and shopping centre occupies a narrow strip facing quays jammed with containers, merchant ships from every corner of the world and a substantial contingent of the Chilean Navy, including former battleships from the Royal Navy made over to Chile after the Falkland Islands Conflict and the barque *Esmeralda*, on which naval cadets are trained by sailing around the world. Rising precipitously behind the port and connected by lifts and gangways or funicular railways is an extraordinary collection of buildings, ranging from dilapidated shacks and chalets to the massive Escuela Naval (Naval Academy) and its sentries with pipeclayed spats, the Museo del Mar Almirante Cochrane, located in the house of that Scots hero of the War of Independence, and elegant restaurants like the Café Turi with its magnificent view of the port below.

THE PEOPLE

Chile's population is 12.8 million, and of this number about 150,000 are indigenous Indians, nearly all of whom live in the forests beyond the Bío Bío River in the south. A fifth is of pure Spanish stock – the descendants of the original colonists are known as Creoles – and most of the remainder is *mestizo*, of mixed blood. Chileans maintain that their climate is the best in the world, their flag the best designed, and their girls the most attractive.

It is remarkable how many of the leading winemakers are of Basque origin – Undurraga, Eyzaguirre, Echenique, Urmeneta, Ochagavía and Errázuriz are all Basque names. Although there is no tradition of wine-making in the wet Basque provinces of Spain, many of the aristocratic descendants of these families, who came to Chile in the 17th and 18th centuries in the service of the Spanish Crown, spearheaded the revival of the wine industry in the mid-19th century.

Later immigration has been on a much smaller scale than in South American countries such as Argentina and Brazil, but the Germans, French, Italians and Swiss, most of whom settled during the 19th century as small-scale farmers in the forest area of the south, have played a part in the country's affairs out of proportion to their numbers. This is particularly true of small specialized groups, such as the French architects, oenologists and restaurateurs, who between them changed the face of Santiago and trans-formed the cuisine and wines.

In the north, the British came in large numbers from the mid-19th century to develop the mining industry and to build railways, and some remained in places like Antofagasta and Iquique. The numerous streets with names like Miller, Cochrane, Mackenna and O'Higgins are not, however, named after these later British settlers but after the English, Scottish and Irish heroes of the War of Independence.

THE ECONOMY

Chile has seen rapid economic growth and significant social change since the ending of the authoritarian regime of General Pinochet in early 1989. One of the most obvious differences is the virtual disappearance of the shanty towns and slums which once ringed the large cities, their inhabitants having been rehoused in small, new homes in neat urban developments.

Unemployment in Chile has sharply declined. This is due to an astonishing increase in economic activity, amounting to 10 percent in 1992 alone. Foreign investment in what is seen as the most stable Latin American country is largely responsible for this change, which is particularly evident on the outskirts of Santiago and other cities where the spanking new factories of international pharmaceutical and electronics companies, as well as huge breweries and soft drink plants, and the countless new packing and refrigeration plants of Dole, United and other food companies, are everywhere to be seen.

Mining (principally nitrate, copper and coal) still leads exports, which totalled US$9,048 million in 1991, followed by manufactured goods and agricultural produce. Wine exports have grown from US$23 million in 1988 to US$119 million in 1992.

VISITING THE WINERIES

Most of the large wineries are within a few hours' drive of Santiago, heading south down the Pan American Highway and turning off either to the right or left (but see the map on page 58). Visitors are always welcome; at Viña Undurraga, for example, the winery and splendid park are open to the public during working hours. Nevertheless, it is advisable to telephone ahead before making a visit. The telephone numbers of individual properties are given in the Wineries section.

At the smaller wineries you will need to speak Spanish; at the large concerns an English-speaking guide or member of the PR staff will show you around the vinification plant and cellars. At Viña Santa Rita a museum is being opened in the historic cellar where General O'Higgins and his followers took refuge during the War of Independence (see pages 89–90), and at the Pirque headquarters of Viña Concha y Toro, there is an elegant reception area and tasting room.

Winemakers are enthusiasts; at Vinícola Torres I have known Miguel Torres himself give up an entire morning to a Californian restaurateur and his wife who had made the long journey from the United States to Curicó, because he felt they were genuinely interested in his venture.

PRACTICALITIES

Outside the airline offices and large hotels in Santiago and Viña del Mar it helps a great deal to speak some Spanish. In rural areas nothing else is spoken although, as mentioned, most of the larger wineries have an English-speaking guide.

There are dozens of good hotels in Santiago and hundreds of restaurants serving French, Italian, Indian, Chinese, Mexican – and even Chilean – food (these last are often known as *picadas*). For listings see that invaluable publication *The South American Handbook*, Chilean guides like *Turis Tel* or a most informative little paper for visitors called *The Latest Daily News*. Outside Santiago there are good hotels in Viña del Mar and some of the other bigger towns. Elsewhere the accommodation is clean but severe with food to match. Most establishments will take the recognized international credit cards. Mealtimes are: breakfast 7.30am to 10am; lunch 1pm to 3pm; dinner from 9pm. (For details of the Chilean cuisine and names of foods and dishes see pages 160–5, and for useful phrases in a restaurant see pages 54–5.)

When shopping, do not miss the open markets, of which there is at least one in every town. Apart from meat, fish, vegetables and flowers, there are stalls selling attractive wickerwork, rugs, pottery and straw hats in every size and shape – from the bowler shape popular with the Incas to sombreros and fine quality panamas.

Chile is not in the tropics and hygiene is generally good, but a few precautions will help to avoid holiday upsets. It is sensible to have injections for typhoid and, for a longer stay and if you are travelling around, for hepatitis B. Santiago water agrees with the Santiaguinos but not with most visitors; ask for bottled water, available either as *agua con gas* or *agua sin gas* (with or without gas) and ensure that it is opened in your presence. In summer you will probably drink a large bottle a day, and remember that there is no point in being particular about bottled water if the ice cubes in your Pisco Sour are made from tap water. If the worst comes to the worst, take Imodium or Lomotil – or ask the chambermaid for an *aguita* (see page 160).

As in all large cities, there are muggers and thieves in Santiago, and areas where it is not advisable to be about on foot at night. Theft can take insidious and unexpected forms, as my wife discovered to her cost in a hotel restaurant when she put her handbag behind her on the chair, only to find that it had been stealthily withdrawn while she ordered! In the face of other incidents of this nature, the official advice of the Hoteliers' Association is to lay handbags on the table and in full sight, and it really *is* important to leave valuables in the hotel safe. A stolen passport and airline tickets take days and endless to-ing and fro-ing to replace.

THE WINEMAKING
TRADITION

Winemaking in Chile began with the Spanish conquest, and that vines were promptly introduced was because the country was occupied in the name of God and the King, and the Catholic priests in their evangelizing mission urgently required wine for the sacraments.

The Spaniards first entered Chile from Peru in 1535, when Diego Almagro, a lieutenant of Pizarro, first reached its heartlands. His stay was short-lived, and it was not until 1541 that Pedro de Valdivia founded Santiago, then pushed further south, where he met fierce resistance from the Mapuche Indians. In the face of repeated insurrections it was not, in fact, until some two centuries later that the far south of the country was peacefully settled.

Although the Conquistadors were disappointed in their search for gold, Chile had other attractions. As one chronicler of the Conquest, the Jesuit Alonso Ovalle, wrote in 1646:

> The climate and soil of Chile are so similar to those of Europe that I find no difference, and in the whole discovery of America no other region is to be found so alike . . . In some, there are winters when it does not rain and does so in the heat of summer; others do not yield wheat or oil, or European fruits cannot be grown. Chile, on the other hand, like Europe, has its six months of spring and summer, and

> another six of autumn and winter; it does not rain in the
> summer but in winter, and all the European fruits and crops
> can also be grown in Chile.

In this Ovalle was echoed by another great 17th-century historian, Diego de Rosales, who wrote that the Maipu region was: 'one vast garden producing wheat, barley, maize, beans, peas and lentils, together with multitudes of trees and an infinity of vines, producing excellent wines.'

There is an intriguing reference by the Abbot of Molina, a very early arrival, to the discovery of black Moscatel growing wild in the foothills of the Andes, but most of the evidence points to vines having been brought from Cuzco in Peru, where they had been introduced from Spain or the Canaries in the mid-16th century by followers of Pedro de Valdivia. According to legend the black País, known elsewhere as the Criolla and in California as the Mission, and still the predominant variety for making everyday wine, was brought to Chile by a Father Francisco Carabantes in 1548.

The first vineyards of which there is a written record belonged to Don Francisco de Aguirre, Corregidor and Chief Justice of the northern town of La Serena. Here and further north in Copiapó, he had planted vineyards by 1551. By 1554 his son-in-law, Juan Jufré, sometimes known as 'the father of Chilean wine', was cultivating vineyards at Macul and Ñuñoa near Santiago. Progress in viticulture further south was chequered. The colonists had planted extensively around the Bío Bío River and Concepción, but in 1576 the Araucanians (as the Spanish now called the rebellious Mapuches) overran the whole area, appropriating the vineyards for making the raw alcoholic *chicha* (see page 42). The settlers retreated north towards Cauquenes and Mataquito, creating large vineyards; one belonging to Diego de León ran to 60,000 plants. These were engulfed by a further Indian uprising in 1655, to the advantage of the northerly vineyards in the region of La Serena, which became the major suppliers to Santiago.

Despite the setbacks in the south, production of wine was now on a scale that threatened exports from Spain, and King Felipe II issued a series of decrees in 1620, 1628, 1631 and 1654 prohibiting new plantations and imposing taxes on existing vineyards. In the wake of the Araucanian uprising of 1655, these regulations were largely ignored. A complaint reached the Queen of Spain, who asked for a report. However, the Governor, supported by the Bishop of Santiago, interceded with her on the grounds of the widespread destruction caused by the Indian rebellions, and at her instigation the Council of the Indies agreed: 'Not to alter that which had always been carried out, namely the planting of vineyards in the Kingdom of Chile.'

Replanting of the vineyards between the Maule and Bío Bío rivers in the south now proceeded with a will and during the 18th century Chile became a major exporter of wines to the other Spanish domains in South America. By the early 19th century the vineyards around Concepción and Cauquenes, still mostly planted with the black País, accounted for two-thirds of all those in the country. Techniques had meanwhile changed little since early colonial days, the simple equipment consisting of a *zaranda de coigue* (wooden sieve), a leather wine press, large earthenware jars for storage and goatskins for transport. Vines were grown low *en vaso* ('goblet-shaped') in Spanish style, and frosts were countered by burning wet straw. In the Central Valley a network of canals was cut during the colonial period to irrigate the vines. The grapes were trodden and fermented whole, fermentation lasting for about 15 days, and the wine was usually sweetened with a syrup made by boiling must. The distillation of skins, pips and defective wine to make *aguardiente* (grape spirit) was carried out from early times (see page 139).

By 1774 exports of wine from Spain to its colonies had so decreased in the face of Chilean competition that yet again a Royal Order was promulgated prohibiting the sale and shipment of Chilean wines. The severity of this measure may be judged by the report of a British naval commander, Captain Basil Hall, in his *Extracts from a Journal written on the Coasts of Chili, Peru and Mexico*, published in 1824:

> Even so late as 1803 . . . orders were received from Spain
> to root up all the vines in the northern provinces, because

the Cadiz merchants complained of a diminution in the consumption of Spanish wines. I was informed at Tepic of a measure precisely similar having a few years earlier been carried into effect in New Galicia, in the case of some extensive and flourishing tobacco plantations. The Americans were prevented, under severe penalties, from raising flax, hemp, or saffron. The culture of the grape and olive was forbidden, as Spain was understood to supply the colonies with wine and oil . . .

No South American could own a ship, nor could a cargo be consigned to him; no foreigner was allowed to reside in the country, unless born in Spain; and no capital, not Spanish, was permitted in any shape to be employed in the colonies. Orders were given, that no foreign vessel, on any pretext whatever, should touch a South American port.

It was the very rigidity of the embargo which resulted first in widespread smuggling and later, as discontent with Spanish rule grew, in a veritable army of foreign volunteers enlisting in the service of the emergent republics. Matters were brought to a head by Napoleon's invasion of Spain and Portugal which, by showing up their military and political impotence, set the colonists on a course that stopped short of nothing but complete independence.

In Chile, the Spanish Captain-General was deposed in 1810 and a junta of seven leading citizens took over from him. In the ensuing hostilities the patriot forces, under the command of John MacKenna and Bernardo O'Higgins, both of Irish descent, scored various successes, but in 1813 the Peruvian Viceroy despatched an army to Concepción and O'Higgins was badly defeated at the Battle of Rancagua in 1814. First taking refuge with 120 of his followers in what are now the cellars of Viña Santa Rita, he subsequently fled with MacKenna to Buenos Aires.

General MacKenna, of whom the well-known wine families of Undurraga and the Eyzaguirres of Los Vascos are direct descendants, was killed in a duel, but O'Higgins lived to fight another day. With José de San Martín he built up a 5,000-strong army, that in 1817 made an epic three-week crossing of the Andes and inflicted decisive defeats on the Royalists at Chacabuco and Maipo. Victory was clinched by the flamboyant Admiral Cochrane, seaman extraordinary and founder of the Chilean navy, who, arriving from England in 1818, and with a motley collection of foreign mercenaries and untried Chilean peasants, attacked and overran the last Spanish stronghold in Chile at Valdivia.

Britain took no direct part in the hostilities, but the ubiquitous presence of the Royal Navy provided the colonists with a shield against outside interference and made possible the commerce which was the lifeblood of the revolution. Independence saw greatly increased trade with the outside world in commodities such as the vast nitrate deposits of the Atacama Desert, copper, silver, gold, coal and agricultural produce, including wine. Foreign mercantile communities sprang up, and British and American engineers built railways. Immigrants began arriving, mainly from Germany, Italy and France; significant among the French were skilled oenologists, without work because of the destruction of the European vineyards by the phylloxera epidemic. An illustrious forerunner was the scientist and agriculturalist Claude Gay who arrived in 1830 and persuaded the government to embark on an experimental station, the Quinta Normal. He also secured the appointment of Luis Sada as its first director, a Genoese who had arrived in Chile after mysterious adventures in Peru. Sada began a programme for acclimatizing plants from abroad, among them about 70 different varieties of vine from France and Italy.

Claude Gay encouraged a group of forward-looking farmers to plant vineyards with varieties from the Quinta Normal, but progress was tentative until 1851, which saw the beginnings of a complete transformation of the wine industry. In the first place this resulted from a visit to France by Don Silvestre Ochagavía, who brought back stocks of some of the best French vine varieties to plant on his estate at Talagante near Santiago. They included Cabernet Sauvignon, Malbec (or Cot), Merlot, Pinot Noir, Riesling, Sauvignonasse and Sémillon. He also engaged a French oenologist, a M Bertrand, to supervise his vineyards. From the outset the vines adapted well and were, in fact, to form the nucleus of the world's only pre-phylloxera clones still in existence. Don Silvestre's visit was shortly followed by that of a trio of vineyard owners: his son-in-law José Tomás Urmeneta, and Maximiano Errázuriz Valdivieso and his son Rafael Errázuriz Urmeneta. The vines brought back by the Errázurizs were planted at Panquehue in the Aconcagua Valley and formed the basis for what was to become the world's largest vineyard, covering an area of some 1,000 hectares.

With the introduction in the mid-19th century by the Pacific Steam Navigation Company of a direct service between Valparaíso and Liverpool, with a call at the port of La Palisse in France, it became the custom for wealthy Chilean mine-owners and agriculturalists to pay long visits to Paris and to educate their children there or in England. Thenceforth, all things French became fashionable in Chile. In the following decades most of the principal buildings in Santiago, such as the Palacio de Bellas Artes, the University of Chile, the railway stations and the central market, were based on French models and often designed by French architects. So, too, were the great houses like the Palacio Cousiño, which were additionally filled with furniture, tapestries and paintings from France.

Nowhere was the French influence more marked than in winemaking. Indeed, it became almost obligatory as a mark of social status for a wealthy owner of a copper or coal mine to invest in a vineyard and to a hire a French oenologist to run it.

The list of those who made the trip to Europe in person to bring back vine stocks reads like a directory of the wine industry and includes: Francisco and Ramón Subercaseaux, Bonifacio and Gregorio Correa Albano (Viña San Pedro), Cristián Lanz (Viña Carmen), Domingo Fernández Concha (Viña Santa Rita), Macario Ossa (Viña Santa Teresa), Luis Pereira (Viña Santa Carolina), Domingo and Melchor Concha y Toro, Louis Cousiño, and Francisco Undurraga.

Had it not been for the whim of those rich Chileans of the late 19th century, the world at large would certainly be poorer in regard to fine wines. Chile was one of the very few areas to escape the phylloxera plague which devastated Europe's vineyards from 1863. This was because, to this day, the phylloxera louse has never penetrated the natural barriers of the Atacama Desert to the north, the wastes of Chilean Antarctica to the south, the Andes to the east and the Pacific to the west. As a result the vines are healthier than grafted stock, last longer – for a century or more – and there is a freer flow of sap, and to propagate them, all that is necessary is to stick a shoot into the ground. So it was that when the European vineyards were replanted with *Vitis vinifera* grafted onto resistant American rootstocks, it was often with noble varieties rescued from Chile.

In his book *Recuerdos de ochenta años*, Don Francisco Undurraga, grandfather of Don Pedro Undurraga, the present head of the firm, has left a particularly vivid account of the lengths to which he went to bring back European vine stocks and obtain oak for his casks.

Don Francisco was especially proud of his 'Vino Rhin' (Riesling). He travelled to Frankfurt, Koblenz and Cologne in the early 1890s to acquire the stocks, which were packed in metal tubes and kept under refrigeration to prevent their budding during the voyage home across the equator. There were enough to plant a hectare in the vineyard at Santa Ana, and the area increased over the years as cuttings were taken.

He was also concerned to age the wine in the best possible fashion and considered that the choicest of all oaks for making casks was Bosnian:

> This wood is first class, and the aroma of the Bosnian oak
> gives the wine a special fragrance which increases with ageing
> and results in an exquisite bouquet unobtainable with any
> other wood.

It so happened that when Don Francisco was appointed Supervisor of the State Railways, he found them in such bad condition as to require the immediate replacement of 50 locomotives and 2,000 flatcars. By a fortunate coincidence, it turned out that the best source of supply for the flatcars was Bosnia and Herzegovina and that the cars were shipped in crates made from Bosnian oak. To continue in his own words:

I knew that the crates were broken up and sold for firewood and offered to buy the staves from the captain of the ship, but he was selling at far too high a price. I then offered him what I thought was reasonable, but he refused and said that at that price he would rather sell them for firewood. I then said: 'Let us ask for a couple of staves from Larios Brothers', and armed with these I was able to demonstrate that each of them was four times the size of his. He answered: 'You are right, señor. I will sell them to you at the price you have offered for firewood', and I bought the lot for 10,000 pesos. The casks were later made for me by the famous cooper L'erromau.

Some of these casks still survive and are being used with excellent results at Viña Undurraga to make its characterful 'Viejo Roble' (see pages 96–7).

The first foreign sale of the 'Vino Rhin' was to a Mr Ear, the managing director of the American Grace & Co. The President of the Republic had been ill and was staying with Don Francisco at his country house – the splendid colonial structure in the gardens adjoining Undurraga's winery. To enliven his convalescence a few friends were invited, including Mr Ear, to whom Don Francisco said that it was his dearest wish that he would buy enough cases of the wine to sell one in every state of the union. Ear bet him a pound sterling that he could not name half of them, at which Don Francisco, who knew his geography, came out with the whole list. For his part, the astonished American undertook to buy 1,000 cases and ensure that 'the splendid Vino Rhin Undurraga' was known in them all. Undurraga was still dealing with Grace & Co in 1943, when American sales had climbed to 55,000 cases.

The year 1903 was a high water mark for the Chilean wine industry, with production rising to a record 275 million litres from 51,400,000 litres in 1883. Exports to Europe had begun in 1877, after the success of Macario Ossa of Viña Santa Teresa at the Vienna International Exhibition in 1873. There were further successes in exhibitions at Bordeaux in 1882, Liverpool in

1885, and the Great Exhibition in Paris in 1889, where the Chilean entry won the Grand Prize. When its wines swept the board at the Buffalo Exhibition in 1910, foreign producers began to take stock of Chile, not simply as an exporter to other Latin American countries, but as a player in the world market.

The euphoria was soon dissipated by the unhelpful stance of successive Chilean governments. The first blow was the Organic Law on Alcohol of 1902, imposing high taxes on wine and spirits. A second Alcohol Law passed in 1938 prohibited new plantings and set a maximum limit on production of 300 million litres of wine per annum. The reasons for this negative attitude appear to have been pressure on the government by the large wine-growing countries and the feeling of the bigger, prestigious Chilean producers that the measures were to their advantage. There was also a growing problem of alcoholism among the working classes, and it was felt that land could be put to better use by growing vegetables and fruit other than grapes. The final blow was the frantic pace of agrarian reform under the Marxist regime of Dr Salvador Allende between 1970 and 1973, when large properties were split up and handed over to smallholders with neither resources nor expertise.

The situation began to improve in 1974, when a law was passed repealing the ban on establishing new vineyards. Subsequent liberalizing legislation in 1979 and 1985 further eased matters for the producers and provided a framework for the modernization of the industry. Indeed, what is striking about current Chilean wine law is the absence of the very detailed rules and regulations enforced in European countries. There are basic stipulations as to the purity and alcohol content of the wine, the use of hybrids and table grapes, and the information on the label, but until a few years ago there were no Denominaciones de Origen (Appellations d'Origine Contrôlée) except for pisco (see page 140) and two fortified wines of minor importance. More recently, five demarcated regions and numerous subregions have been set up for the beverage wines, which must be labelled accordingly. A summary of the current wine law, the Reglamenta Ley of 1986, can be found on pages 176–8.

After visiting Chile in 1984, I wrote that: 'Perhaps the most pressing problem today is a lack of capital to modernize the wineries, many of which, especially the cooperatives, are thoroughly old-fashioned in their equipment. To a foreign observer, the most urgent need would seem to be the replacement of innumerable picturesque, but insanitary wooden vats and barrels, long past their useful life and actually detrimental to the wine which is aged in them.' Since then the Chilean wine industry has undergone the most radical change since its renaissance in the 19th century.

Following the lead of the Spanish winemaker Miguel Torres, who acquired a winery near Curicó in 1978 and at once began equipping it with stainless steel fermentation tanks and small oak casks, the large firms began installing stainless steel and oak barriques from France and the USA. Now, there is hardly a bodega in Chile with any claim to producing fine wines without its temperature-controlled stainless steel vats, modern presses, cooling equipment and small oak casks – at one end of the scale Viña Santa Rita has bought 8,000 of them.

All this, together with the planting of extensive new vineyards with noble varieties, has required huge investment. Much has come from a new generation of industrialists, which has taken as much pride in planting or replanting vineyards and modernizing the wineries as did the 19th-century mine-owners. Such is Don Ricardo Claro Valdés, a prominent Chilean financier, who now owns both Viña Santa Rita and Viña Carmen and who has gone to great lengths to bring the wines up to international standards. If the old family owners have in some cases given way to corporations and limited companies, in others a bargain has been struck, as with Viña Los Vascos, where the Eyzaguirre family sold a 50 percent share to Château Lafite, but retains a lively interest in the making of the wines.

With sales of fine wines now targeted at the USA and Europe rather than the Latin American market, another most significant development has been the emergence of well-equipped, medium-sized or 'boutique' wineries making varietal wines in the Californian or Australian manner and destined almost entirely for export. Some belong to farmers who in the past sold their crops to the large firms, but who have now installed modern winemaking equipment and are selling wines under their own label. This, in turn, has resulted in the majors extending their vineyards so as to become self-sufficient in grapes, so that increasing amounts of wine are estate-grown and -bottled.

There is also in Chile an increasing awareness of the importance of *terroir* and of growing the different grape varieties where the soils and climate best suit them – this is, of course, reflected in the emergent demarcated regions. For example, Chardonnay is now being grown near Cauquenes in the cooler south, where the vineyards are open to Pacific breezes, and a new and favoured locality for growing white wines is the Casablanca area near Valparaíso, which has much in common with the Napa Valley in the USA. There are also plans to revive wine-growing in the Bío Bío area in the south where the Spaniards planted some of their most extensive vineyards. Here, the research corporation Fundación Chile is experimenting with drip irrigation and is building a modern demonstration winery in an area where viticulture was dying out.

All in all, the last decade has seen a striking improvement in the quality of Chilean wines, especially the fresh and fruity young whites, which have benefited most from cold fermentation and modern techniques. But this is not only the outcome of modern equipment; a new generation of lively young oenologists has travelled and studied abroad in France, Australia and California. Numbers of foreign oenologists have also come, intrigued by a country which has always been known for its superb fruit, if not for matching quality in its wines. Hugh Ryman and his team, for example, spend the winemaking period in Chile, while others have decided to settle permanently.

Exports of bottled wine have grown from 9,064,228 litres in 1984 to 96,028,356 litres in 1993 – a staggering increase of some 1,000 percent. Chilean wines are also receiving awards at all the major international exhibitions, one of the most impressive successes being that of a Cabernet Sauvignon at the Gault-Millau Olympiad in Paris, where it outpointed all comers, including First Growths from France itself.

There is an unmistakable air of confidence about the young oenologists who now have both the training and the equipment to make the most of the grapes which Hugh Johnson once described as: 'one of the earth's great natural resources.'

ANATOMY OF CHILEAN WINE

THE REGIONS

Grape growing in Chile extends from the latitudes of 27° 30' to 30° 00' or about 1,200 kilometres (750 miles) from north to south. Over this long distance there are great differences in soil and climate, and there are four broad geographical zones: Zona Norte, Zona Pisquera, Zona de Riego and Zona de Secano.

1 ZONA NORTE (NORTHERN ZONE)

This zone extends from the arid deserts of the extreme north to the basin of the River Copiapó, embracing Regions I and II and part of Region III. There is little viticulture in the far north because of the intense heat, but thanks to drip irrigation sizeable amounts of table grapes are grown around Copiapó, as are small quantities of Moscatel for making pisco.

2 ZONA PISQUERA (PISCO ZONE)

This demarcated area, in which the aromatic native brandy, pisco, is produced from Moscatel grapes, covers part of Region III and all of Region IV. Because of the zone's mountainous terrain, the vines are grown only in the broad valleys of the principal rivers, the Huasco, Elqui, Limarí and Choapa, running from the Andes towards the Pacific, and on the slopes of their tributaries' smaller valleys. Substantial amounts of table grapes, especially Flame Seedless, are also grown. See the Pisco chapter for further details.

3 ZONA DE RIEGO (IRRIGATED ZONE)

This is the heartland of Chilean wine production and extends from the Aconcagua basin north of Santiago to the basin of the Bío Bío River some 650 kilometres (400 miles) to the south. It is bounded by the Andes to the east and the foothills of the Cordillera de la Costa or coastal mountains to the west and forms the great central depression of the country, embracing the irrigated areas of Regions V, VI, VII and VIII, part of Region IX, and the Metropolitan Region. It is crossed by a mountain chain north of Santiago, beyond which is the Aconcagua Valley. Other mountain chains to the south of the capital mark the southern limit of the Maipo Region and delimit the Cachapoal and Colchagua subregions.

Further south of this the Central Valley widens; there are no further mountain barriers; and the coastal range, 600–800 metres (1,800–2,400 feet) high for most of its length, is lower in the south and broken by wide valleys, which by allowing exposure to cooling Pacific breezes significantly modify the climate. The limits for growing grapes are 1,000 metres (3,000 feet) above sea level in the Andes to the east and 600 metres (1,800 feet) in the Cordillera de la Costa to the west.

The main geographical feature of the Central Valley is the series of rivers which cross it from their sources in the Andes on the way to the sea. The larger are the Aconcagua, Mapocho, Maipo, Cachapoal, Tinguiririca, Teno, Lontué, Claro, Maule, Ñuble and Bío Bío. It is these rivers and their tributaries which feed the canals needed to irrigate the vineyards during the dry, hot summers.

Some 41 percent (26,000 hectares) of vineyards growing grapes for wine, including most of the high quality bottled wine, lie within this Irrigated Zone. The most important red grapes, which account for 52 percent of plantations, are Cabernet Sauvignon, Malbec and Merlot; the main white grapes are Sémillon, Sauvignon, Chardonnay and different varieties of Moscatel.

Decree Laws of 1979 and 1985 established the demarcated regions and subregions, listed on page 32 from north to south, within the Irrigated Zone (descriptions can be found in the Wineries section, pages 56–138).

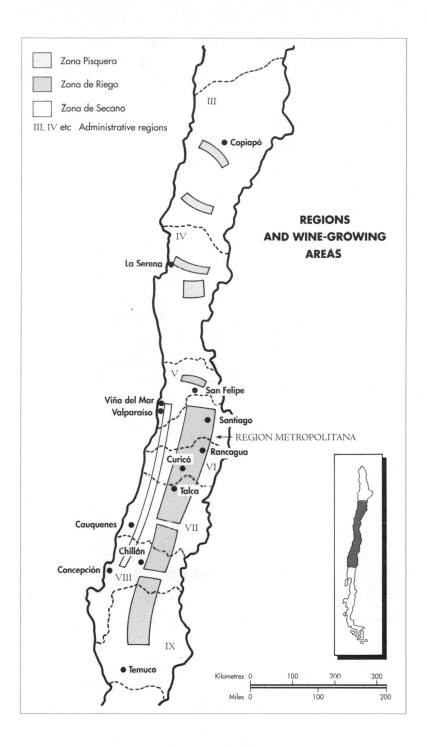

Zona Pisquera

Zona de Riego

Zona de Secano

III, IV etc   Administrative regions

III

● Copiapó

REGIONS
AND WINE-GROWING
AREAS

IV

La Serena ●

V

● San Felipe

Viña del Mar ●
Valparaíso ●

● Santiago

←— REGION METROPOLITANA

● Rancagua

Curicó ●

VI

Talca ●

Cauquenes ●

VII

Chillán ●

Concepción ●

VIII

IX

● Temuco

Kilometres 0   100   200   300

Miles 0   100   200

Aconcagua Region	Maule Region
Panquehue	Curicó
Casablanca	Lontué
	Molina
Maipo Region	Sagrada Familia
Isla de Maipo	Talca
Santiago	San Clemente
Pirque	San Javier
Buin	Linares
Santa Ana	Cauquenes
Llano de Maipo	Parral
	Villa Alegre
Rapel Region	
Rancagua	**Bío Bío Region**
Rengo	Ñuble
Peumo	Chillán
San Fernando	Coelemu
Colchagua	Quillón
Santa Cruz	Yumbel
Cachapoal	
Chimbarongo	
Nancagua	
Tinguiririca	

4 ZONA DE SECANO (UNIRRIGATED ZONE)

This comprises three subzones. The first runs parallel to the Central Valley along the coastal mountains from Valparaíso in the north down to Coelemu near Concepción; the second is around the town of Cauquenes and takes in an inland spur of the Cordillera de la Costa; the third lies south of the Ñuble.

In all of these areas, which between them account for 58 percent of Chile's vineyards, there is sufficient rainfall for vines to be grown without irrigation. The predominant grape is the black País, introduced by the early Spanish colonists, which is grown low and pruned *en cabeza* ('goblet-shaped', the Chilean term for *en vaso*), and cultivated by a host of smallholders, who take their fruit to the cooperatives to be vinified. The yield per hectare is low, although the southern areas are more densely planted than any others in Chile.

In irrigated areas the País fruits prolifically, giving rise to very ordinary bulk wines, but in the south of the Unirrigated Zone, with yields as low as 3,000 litres per hectare, the wine makes pleasant everyday drinking.

Small amounts of Riesling, Sauvignon Blanc, Chardonnay and Moscatel are grown in the south of the zone, and field studies undertaken by the government experimental station at Cauquenes and by Fundación Chile (see page 79) have shown that with supplementary drip irrigation and up-to-date vinification methods, the area can produce both red and white wines as good as those of the Central Valley.

SOILS AND CLIMATE

A cross-section of the Central Valley shows that it is a wide basin, into which a mass of debris from the mountains which flank it has been carried down by glacial and gravitational action; in some places this debris is up to 90 metres (300 feet) deep. The valley is young in geological terms, and is sedimentary in character.

The most widespread type of soil, and among the best for growing vines, is mildly alkaline and made up of limestone, clay and small stones, allowing for good drainage. Also typical of the Central Valley is the alluvial silt and sand of the river margins. At the eastern side of the valley, especially in the Maule Region around Talca and Curicó and along the foothills of the Andes, there is a belt of volcanic ash, slightly acidic, with a high content of organic material, and loam-like in texture with good drainage. At the opposite side of the valley in the Maule and Bío Bío regions in the foothills of the coastal range, the land is very much broken up and the soils are granitic and slightly acid. The loam of hill slopes is topped with quartz gravel, while the valleys, sometimes called 'bogs' because of the poor drainage, are alluvial.

The climate varies widely over the long length of the wine-growing area. Generally described as Mediterranean, it ranges from arid in the Pisco and Aconcagua regions to semi-arid in Maipo, subhumid in Rapel, and humid in Maule and Bío Bío. Similarly, the average annual rainfall and temperature vary from 250–400 millimetres and 15–16°C (59–61°F) in Aconcagua to 1,200–1,500 millimetres and 13–14°C (55–57°F) in Bío Bío. Over most of the Central Valley there is insufficient rainfall for viticulture, so the vines are irrigated in spring and summer. This is usually done by diverting water from one of the many rivers into irrigation channels and then into furrows in the vineyards. In recent years drip irrigation has also been used, each plant being fed individually from a perforated tube. This has the advantage that if there is a deficiency of nutrients or minerals, they can be dissolved and fed to the plants in the correct amounts.

Special climatic factors also affect the quality of the grapes. With the Andes towering above the vineyards, its peaks snow-covered throughout the year, volumes of cold air flow into the Central Valley during the night. This results in a sharp fall from daytime temperatures of 30–35°C (85–95°F) during the summer to 10–15°C (50–59°F) at night and, by reducing respiration at night, promotes the accumulation of sugar in the grapes as well as the synthesis of polyphenols (tannins and colouring matter) and the substances responsible for the aroma of the fruit.

The first thing one notices on a visit to Chile is the brilliance and clarity of the light, which seems to bring the Andes even closer than they are and makes colours luminous and glowing. In summer, there is virtually no cloud or rain – each morning one wakes to a perfect sunny day. The dazzling light enhances photosynthesis and growth, so that Miguel Torres, with vineyards in both Catalonia and Chile, has noted that in the Penedès there is a span of six months between budding and harvesting of the vines, whereas in his Curicó vineyards the interval is only five and a half months.

Near the coast and in wide valleys, like those of the Elqui and Aconcagua running down to the sea, the climate is much affected by the cold Humboldt Current flowing off-shore in the Pacific. This cools the lower layers of the

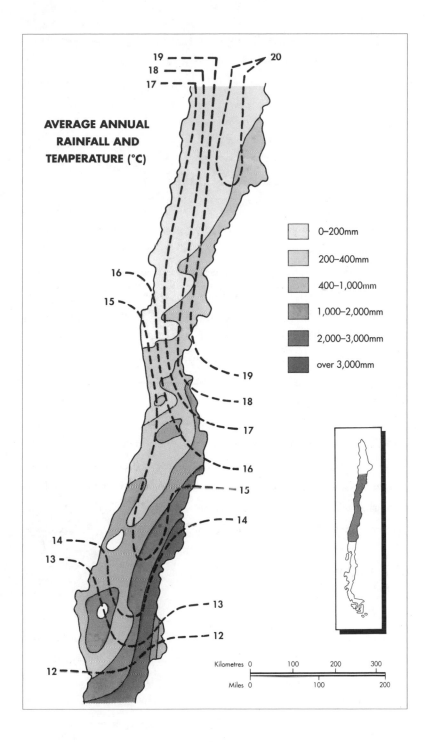

AVERAGE ANNUAL
RAINFALL AND
TEMPERATURE (°C)

0–200mm

200–400mm

400–1,000mm

1,000–2,000mm

2,000–3,000mm

over 3,000mm

Kilometres 0   100   200   300

Miles 0   100   200

atmosphere, giving rise to low cloud and fogs known as *camanchacas*, which penetrate inland (see also page 142). There is a similar flow of cold air at the southern end of the Cordillera de la Costa, where the mountains are lower and broken up. In fact, climatic conditions in the Cauquenes and Casablanca areas, at opposite ends of the Cordillera, resemble those of the Napa Valley and Sonoma County in California in being almost perfect for viticulture.

VINE VARIETIES

In the unirrigated area, the only grape of practical importance for red wines is the País, which accounts for 85 percent of plantations. Although grown in much smaller amounts, the white varieties are actually better suited to ecological conditions; they are basically Sémillon, Sauvignon Blanc, Torontel and various varieties of Moscatel. The Irrigated Zone of the Central Valley is planted with a variety of the noble vines brought in the first place from Europe in the 19th century. They are not grafted, since Chile has never suffered from phylloxera, and are planted in the proportion of 52 percent of red vines to 48 percent of white. In the past, different varieties were often planted together in the proportions in which they were used in the wines, *coupage* being effected in the vineyard, as was once the case in Rioja. With the present emphasis on varietal wines, all new plantings are of single vine varieties.

In recent years there has been a shortfall of grapes for making white wine. To meet this, the wine laws have been relaxed and it is now permissible to make white wines with table grapes such as the Sultanina and Flame Seedless. The wines must, however, be labelled as such, and they are not exported.

RED GRAPES

País

The País, also known as the Criolla and in California as the Mission, was the first to be introduced to Chile, being widely planted by the Spanish settlers. It still occupies some 32 percent of the total vineyard area and is the principal grape of the Unirrigated Zone, where it produces sound enough wine for everyday drinking. When it is irrigated, prolific fruiting results in much poorer quality. The widely drunk *chicha* (see page 42) and unfiltered *vino pipeño* (see page 43) are both made from País.

Cabernet Sauvignon

First introduced from Bordeaux in the mid-19th century, the Cabernet soon established itself as the grape *par excellence* for fine reds. It accounts for 32 percent of all plantings and is the predominant red grape in the irrigated Central Valley, the best wines perhaps coming from Maipo, Cachapoal and Curicó.

Malbec

The Malbec is the most widely planted red grape after the País and Cabernet Sauvignon, accounting for 5.7 percent of the total vineyard area. Not much seen on the labels of exported wines, Malbec blended with Merlot and Verdot is sold in Chile as Vino Burdeos ('Bordeaux').

Merlot

Chile grows excellent Merlot, especially in the southern part of the Central Valley. Its planting makes up 1.8 percent and it is increasingly being vinified and bottled as a varietal in its own right.

Pinot Noir

Very little Pinot Noir is grown (it represents only 0.3 percent of the total) because of its low yields. Nevertheless, Viña Undurraga makes an attractive wine, widely available in Chile in the distinctive flagon-shaped *caramayolas*, and Viña Valdivieso is growing sizeable amounts in the Lontué area for use in its best sparkling wines.

Other red grapes

Small amounts of other red grapes are grown. Carignan, a native of the Midi in southern France, makes up 1.4 percent of the total, and is sometimes grown in the unirrigated areas where it makes wines rather deeper in colour and more intense in flavour than the ubiquitous País.

WHITE GRAPES

Sémillon

Sémillon is by far the most widely planted of the white grapes, accounting for 26.3 percent of the total vineyard area. It is often blended, especially with Sauvignon Blanc, and has the reputation of making rather dull wines on its own. This is not my own experience. When cold fermented and expertly made, as at Viña Cánepa, the wines can be flowery and refreshing.

Moscatel

Moscatel has been cultivated since colonial times and there is even a legend that a black Moscatel grew wild in the foothills of the Andes. Very large amounts are used in the Pisco Zone for making pisco, for which some eight varieties are grown, notably Moscatel de Alejandría, Moscatel rosada and Moscatel de Austria. The grape also produces a fragrant white table wine in the Unirrigated Zone's far south. It accounts for about 6 percent of all white grapes.

Sauvignon Blanc

Sauvignon Blanc and Chardonnay are the two most popular of the new generation of cold-fermented fruity and fragrant white varietals. Sauvignon Blanc is, in fact, grown to a larger extent (it makes up 4.6 percent of the total) than any white grape other than Sémillon and Moscatel. However, many of the Chilean wineries do not, like Santa Carolina, Torres and Cánepa, have real Sauvignon but Sauvignonasse, which gives good aroma and flavour, but not the gooseberry and herbal taste of the original.

Chardonnay

Although most of the wineries are now producing cold-fermented Chardonnay for export, extremely little of it has been grown until recently. Now that

Cabernet and Chardonnay are the most fashionable of wines, the situation is rapidly changing and the producers are hastening to plant. The wines are fragrant and lighter than most from elsewhere, the best coming from the new Casablanca subregion near Valparaíso and from Cauquenes in the south.

Riesling

Little Riesling is grown, despite Chile's first great success in exporting white wine with the Undurraga 'Rhin' in 1903. Undurraga continues to make a good Riesling from vines derived from the original stocks brought from Germany in the early 1890s. Miguel Torres makes a delicate blend of Riesling and Gewürztraminer – another very scarce grape.

Other white grapes

Other white grapes include the Torontel and the Pedro Jiménez, the sherry grape, grown in the Pisco Region.

Current (1993) percentages for the areas (in hectares) planted with vines producing *only* for export differ significantly from those given above and reflect the increasing plantation of Chardonnay, Sauvignon Blanc and Merlot:

Chardonnay	1,984.3 ha	11.8%
Sauvignon Blanc	4,553.1 ha	27.0%
Riesling	252.7 ha	1.5%
Chenin Blanc	25.4 ha	0.15%
Total	**6,815.5 ha**	**40.45%**
Cabernet Sauvignon	7,976.4 ha	47.6%
Merlot	1,012.8 ha	6.0%
Malbec	789.2 ha	4.7%
Pinot Noir	106.1 ha	0.6%
Petit Verdot	44.9 ha	0.3%
Total	**9,929.4 ha**	**59.2%**

CULTIVATION

The most striking difference between viticulture in Chile and that of the other important wine-growing areas of the world is that the vines have never been affected by that voracious pest, phylloxera. This, as has been explained, is because of the remoteness of the country and the existence of natural barriers. The most stringent precautions are in force to prevent the entry of infected vine stocks, and material imported from abroad is subject to long quarantine. Freedom from phylloxera obviates the use of resistant root-stocks and grafting, and vines may be planted simply by inserting shoots into the ground.

In the Unirrigated Zone, the predominant País vine is cultivated as it has been for centuries. It is grown low and unsupported and pruned *en cabeza*, by leaving three main branches, each with two shoots, which produce 12 bunches of grapes in all.

The technique of the smallholders is of the simplest. Animals are used for tilling and other operations, and fumigation is confined to the treatment of oidium, or powdery mildew (*Uncinula necator*), and the riddance of a small red spider, the *arañita roja* (*Brevipalpus chilensis*), peculiar to Chile. In some of the wet valleys in the south, the so-called *vegas* or 'bogs', the vines are kept clear of the ground by training on *espalderas* as used in the irrigated areas of the Central Valley.

This traditional method trains the vines Bordeaux fashion on wires supported by stakes; the trellises are normally 1.3–1.7 metres (4–5.5 feet) high with 0.8–2 metres (2.5–6.5 feet) between rows. The usual method of pruning is the double Guyot, leaving two lateral branches with 8–12 buds each, and another smaller branch with three or four buds to provide for the next year's growth.

Using this system, average yield varies between 7,000 and 11,000 kilograms per hectare (conversion to hectolitres of wine is not at all simple, but these figures correspond to a range of between 4,000 and 8,000 hectolitres per hectare).

A modification of this system, introduced from California, is a high trellis (1.8–2 metres/6–6.5 feet) with one or two crosspieces at the top. The rows are distanced at 2.5–4 metres (8–13 feet) to allow for the use of tractors, and yield is more or less doubled unless controlled in the interests of making good quality wines.

A third system of training was introduced in about 1950 from Argentina, in the first place for growing vines for the exclusive production of table grapes. The stakes are much higher and the vines form a pergola with a dense canopy of leaves on top and bare stems below. The system is known as the *parronal*, or somewhat quaintly, as I have seen nothing like it in Spain except for the rustic arbours of Galicia, as the *parral español* or 'Spanish system'. It proved such a success with table grapes, lending itself to mechanization and leading to very high yields of as much as 40,000 kilograms per hectare, that in the mid-1970s it was extended to vines providing grapes for winemaking. To begin with, it was claimed that the quality of the wine was not affected, and grapes grown in *espalderas* and *parronales* were often mixed. However, it later became clear that wine made with fruit from the *parronales* developed unpleasant herbal aromas and lacked flavour and intensity.

Parronales continue to be used extensively for growing table grapes and in the Pisco Region for the grapes used in making the base wine for distillation. It is now generally accepted that the fine wines are best made with fruit grown in *espalderas* and that where the Californian system is used, yields must be controlled. As in Europe, a rule of thumb limit of 5,000 litres per hectare is often mentioned, but it would seem that, given irrigation and Chilean conditions, this may be exceeded. It depends, as James Halliday and Hugh Johnson pointed out in *The Art and Science of Wine*, on the judgement and skill of the grower and on local conditions.

Chile is mercifully free from most vineyard diseases and pests, in partic-ular phylloxera, as has been noted. The only two diseases to pose any problem are oidium, against which the vines are dusted with sulphur from the time of budding until late spring, and botrytis, or 'noble rot'. The vines are to some extent affected by nematodes, because self-rooted *Vitis vinifera* is more prone to attack by worms of this sort than American stocks. The most serious insect pests are the tiny red vine spider and, more damaging, the ground pearl (*Margarodes vitis*), which is especially prevalent in the Maipo Region and which attacks the vine roots. No remedy has yet been found, other than a proposal to graft onto American rootstocks.

THE WINE HARVEST

Harvesting of table grapes begins early and lasts, according to the region, from November to April. The harvesting of the pisco grapes, grown in the special microclimate of the Andean valleys of the north, is also extended, lasting from mid-February until the end of May. Harvesting in the Central Valley of grapes for making wine begins in late February for early ripening varieties such as Chardonnay and lasts until the end of April for Cabernet Sauvignon. The País grown in the unirrigated areas of the south is an even later variety, and picking continues until the beginning of May.

At the time of writing, only one winery, Viña Concha y Toro, is using a mechanical harvester. The normal practice is to pick the grapes by hand into plastic boxes, which are then emptied into trucks or trailers lined with plastic sheeting, for conveyance to the winery. It is increasingly common for fine white varietals, such as Sauvignon Blanc and Chardonnay, fermented at low temperature to preserve fragrance and fruit, to be picked in the very early morning so as to arrive cool at the winery.

Chile, like other wine-growing countries, has its harvest festivals, and two potions are much drunk at these times. *Chicha* is a Quechuan word, and the Incas made this brew by fermenting maize. Later on, the rebellious Mapuches, tired of uprooting the colonists' vines, began picking the grapes and allowing them to ferment, thus making a homespun wine. Today, *chicha* is simply used to describe must or partly fermented grape juice. If fermentation has only just begun, the drink is known as *chicha cruda* and is very sweet, tasting much like raspberry vinegar. Attempts, inevitably unsuccessful, are sometimes made to stabilize it by cooking. It is then known as *chicha cocida* — and should be avoided.

Vino pipeño is a new wine which has not been filtered or clarified and contains all the dead yeasts and solid residue from the grapes. Rodrigo Alvarado Moore, the distinguished Chilean agronomist and wine writer, once said that it may also contain a variety of other things: 'beginning with soil and ending with other unsuspected ingredients best left undescribed.' You have been warned!

MAKING AND MATURING THE WINE

Writing in 1987, Rodrigo Alvarado Moore had severe things to say about the Chilean wine industry:

> In general it may be affirmed that there is little correspondence in Chile between the prodigality of nature in providing grapes for wine and the level of technology in the country's wineries. Nevertheless, there is an important and select number of oenologists, most of them also agronomists, trained in the three Chilean universities with agronomy departments.
>
> It would require complex analysis, historical, economic and political to explain the causes of this discrepancy between levels of technology in viticulture and viniculture in all its aspects . . .

Sr Alvarado goes on to list some of the immediate reasons for the 'discrepancy' as being that only about 10 percent of wine is sold in bottles of less than a litre, most of it being destined for 5-litre carafes or sold direct from the barrel by smallholders to the consumer. Again, until recently, new bottles were used solely for export wines, wines for domestic consumption being sold only against the return of the bottle. Further than this, the large firms relied heavily on clumsily made wine bought from smallholders, and even in their own bodegas often aged the wines in large and ancient vats made of raulí. This native South American beech (*Nothofagus procera*), tended to impart disagreeable odours and flavours.

It should be said at this point that there have been sweeping changes during the last half-dozen years. More and more, the large firms are planting vineyards and aiming at self-sufficiency in regard to grapes, while the plant for vinifying the wine and the capacity for maturing it in new oak casks from France and the USA are rapidly becoming the equal of anything elsewhere.

Until these recent changes, the methods of winemaking in Chile were basically those of the French oenologists engaged by the 19th-century mineowners and agriculturalists at the time when they replanted the vineyards with noble varieties from Europe. The wineries, such as those of Santa Carolina, Errázuriz and Undurraga, were designed by top-flight French architects, and even today the deep cellars, with their double walls and temperature changes varying by only a degree or two throughout the year, could scarcely be improved. The state-of-the-art *fin de siècle* Bordeaux technology could hardly be better exemplified than by the narrow gauge railway constructed by Cousiño Macul to take the grapes direct from the vineyards into the heart of the bodega.

One of the most significant developments has been the replacement of the large wooden fermentation vats with stainless steel tanks, cooled either by running water over the outside or by an internal coil through which a refrigerant is pumped. Apart from being much more hygienic this allows the wines to be vinified more slowly at optimum temperatures, at around 25–28°C (77–82°F) for the reds and 15–18°C (59–64°F) for the whites, thus retaining as much as possible of the fruity taste and aroma of the grapes.

It was the custom, as in the Spanish Rioja, to age red wines for long years in wood. This took place not in the small 225-litre barriques of Bordeaux or *barricas* of Rioja, but in very large barrels, sometimes made of oak, but generally of raulí, which does not give the same pleasant vanilla-like aroma and flavour. More seriously, these large barrels, although often having a small hatch at the bottom through which a man may climb, were difficult to clean, and the use of sulphur candles or sulphur dioxide could lead to traces of sulphuric acid being left in the wood. Only too often the net result was that splendidly fresh and fruity young wine became progressively staler in *cubas* and *fudres* which should long ago have been retired. In some cases, otherwise beautiful old wines were rendered undrinkable by the presence of mercaptans (penetratingly unpleasant organic sulphur compounds).

Tastes have changed in favour of younger and fruitier red wines and, at least in the large wineries and with red wines destined for export, current practice is to mature them for only six months or a year in small casks of new oak imported from France or the USA. They are then aged for a year or so in bottle before release. Where raulí vats are still used, it is usually for fermentation or holding the wine during malolactic fermentation, and they are normally so coated with tartrate as not to affect the flavour.

Chile has been best known for its red wines, especially Cabernet Sauvignon, which has taken so well to its adopted home. The domestic taste for white wines was, as formerly in Spain, for heavily oaked (and sometimes maderized) wine. Again, there has been a sea change, wrought both by the worldwide demand for young, fruity varietal white wines and by the influence of the many young Chilean oenologists who have trained in California and completed their studies by working in Australia, New Zealand and elsewhere.

It is here that the use of cooling equipment, pneumatic presses of the Bucher type, vacuum filters and above all temperature-controlled fermentation in stainless steel has had the most dramatic effect. It is now standard practice to crush the grapes then macerate them before fermentation by allowing the skins to remain in contact with the must in a tank, so allowing for the must to be permeated by aromatic substances in the skins. Low temperatures permit longer maceration, especially when the grapes are picked and delivered to the winery early in the morning.

Malolactic fermentation, which reduces acidity, is not usually desirable in white wines. They are therefore treated with sulphur dioxide to kill off the yeasts immediately after fermentation and are then left for a few months to clarify before being filtered and bottled. Some white wines are aged for up to six months in small oak barrels, which gives them a more complex bouquet, but because the aim is generally to preserve the young, flowery fragrance of the fresh grapes, most are not.

Chardonnay is a special case. When cold fermented in stainless steel and without malolactic fermentation, well-made new generation Chilean wines have a remarkably vivid nose and taste of tropical fruit – lichees, melon, pineapple and the like. However, when fermented in small oak casks in traditional fashion, they develop a deeper, rounder, 'buttery' flavour, and this is actually enhanced by allowing malolactic fermentation to proceed.

Sparkling wine, uninhibitedly known in Chile as 'champagne' or '*champaña*' in the absence of any agreement with the producers in Reims, is made both by the champagne method and by the Charmat process in *cuves closes*. The best, such as Valdivieso's 'Nature', is made from a 50:50 blend of Pinot Noir and Chardonnay by the traditional method of second fermentation in bottle with a long spell in cool cellars. It is dry and biscuity, with lovely fruit and good mousse. Some of the wines made in bulk by the Charmat process in refrigerated and pressurized tanks, like Concha y Toro's 'Subercaseaux', are also good of their kind, the Moscatel being particularly refreshing during the hot Chilean summer.

CHARACTERISTICS AND CLASSIFICATION

When I first visited Chile, some ten years ago, a start had not yet been made on demarcating beverage wines. At the time, most Chileans, and wine waiters in particular, believed implicitly that the older the wine the better it was, and the only scheme for classifying wines depended on this. They were divided into five categories, the first being those which had spent three or more years in American oak and one in bottle. These were usually named after members of the aristocracy. The reds contained 100 percent Cabernet Sauvignon and the whites a blend of Sauvignon Blanc and Sémillon from the Central Valley. At the other end of the scale were cooperative reds made from the País grape and lower quality Sémillon whites.

I found at the time that some of the 'first division' red wines were over-oaky and drying out, or even smelt and tasted of mercaptan, and that I often preferred the younger third and fourth category wines. This last category dated from the days when the government insisted that producers sell certain wines at official and artificially low prices and was known as 'Gran Vino'. About three years old, the wine was generally round and fruity.

Chilean wines mature more quickly than European, and in view of the current taste for younger, fruity red wines, even the *reservas* and *gran reservas* are now often no more than four years old (incidentally there is no definition of either a *reserva* or *gran reserva* in terms of the period spent in cask and bottle; they are simply wines regarded by the winery as its best). The old five categories have therefore fallen into abeyance, and where the names of the first category survive, such as the famous 'Antiguas Reservas' from Cousiño Macul or 'Marqués de Casa Concha' from Concha y Toro, the time in oak has been much reduced, to my mind to the benefit of the wines.

As regards the earlier release of the red wines, there is a reverse side to the coin. No-one could criticize them on the score of the intense fruit in the nose and taste or of good balance of oak and fruit in those aged in small casks; what they tend to lack is the complexity of a good claret or burgundy. Complexity is, of course, achieved by bottle age, and there is no short cut.

In this connection I wrote to Douglas Murray of Discover Wine, makers of the excellent 'Montes', about his winemaking credo and the future for Chilean wines. He sent me this interesting reply:

> While at San Pedro, Aurelio Montes and I started what was called 'Castillo de Molina', being the first to import French barrels to Chile and visualizing a true quality wine as a result of our efforts. Everyone seemed puzzled at our insistence on quality as an objective. The result was that the first two vintages were sold to the Napa Valley top producer Caymus as 'Liberty School' (a milestone) and the balance exported to France as 'Castillo de Molina'. We made our point and had mapped the route we wanted to follow . . .
>
> My belief about winemaking is that we are in a permanent, obsessive search for the ultimate Chilean wine and only experimentation will lead to perfection. Very

simply, I would love to see us as the creators of the first Chilean 'Grange Hermitage', and our 'Montes Alpha' is the first step in that direction.

As regards the white wines, the old categories have gone completely by the board. I can think of only one wine in the traditional oaky style, Undurraga's 'Viejo Roble'. For this I confess a weakness; it is well made and fresh despite the time spent in oak and is along the lines of the oak-aged Riojas now coming into fashion again after a spell in the wilderness. As noted, some of the whites are in fact matured briefly in small oak, making them less immediately fragrant, but resulting in greater complexity and longer life.

Virtually all the whites are now fresh and fruity young varietal wines, lighter than California's and the best of them much in the style of the Marlborough wines from New Zealand. There is indeed a remarkable similarity. In comparative tastings, I have found the Chilean wines somewhat lighter and more flowery, developing a peachy nose and flavour in the glass, while the New Zealand whites are firmer, with more body, and retain the original nose and taste to the end.

By no means all the new-style whites attain this high standard. During a recent visit to Chile, my wife and I must have tasted some 200 white wines. Too many were light and clean but suffered from lack of nose and flavour, or started with fragrance and fruit which fairly soon disappeared in the glass. I have questioned two leading oenologists, Miguel Torres and Ignacio Recabarren, about this. It seems that the causes are varied.

Modern technology has revolutionized Chilean wineries, but not all the winemakers have yet learned to take advantage of the pristine stainless steel and new oak casks. Both oenologists agree that high yields drastically affect quality and should not exceed 10,000 litres per hectare, whereas in the Central Valley yields of 14,000–18,000 litres per hectare are common. In view of the high summer temperatures, better wines could be made if more of the wineries picked the grapes early in the morning and if more attention was given to matters such as maceration of the fruit, the period of ageing and time of bottling, rather than to rapid throughput and early clearing and sterilization of clean, but neutral commercial wines. As mentioned earlier, Sauvignon Blanc is a special case, since unlike Santa Carolina, Torres and Cánepa, many of the Chilean wineries do not have real Sauvignon, but Sauvignonasse, which gives good aroma and flavour, but not the gooseberry and herbal taste and the crispness of the original.

Because of the benign climate and months of cloudless sunny weather in summer, there is generally little to choose between vintages. There are of course upsets, even in this demi-paradise for wine-growers. For example, quite untypical frosts in the spring (September–October) of 1991 drastically affected most of the vines in the Casablanca subregion and those in the Central Valley growing east of the Pan American Highway; consequently yields in 1992 were much reduced. When asked about this, Miguel Torres explained that in general the quality of the 1992 vintage was not affected by the frosts, since the decrease in yield per hectare in some cases *improved* the quality of the wine.

Naturally, individual producers have their exceptional vintages – and 1993 was an excellent year for white wines in general – but there are none of the charts and plastic cards so popular in countries with more fickle climes.

PRODUCERS AND EXPORTERS

Chile has relatively few large wineries, but those few are *very* large, comparable in size to the biggest in Europe and California, with the exception of Gallo. The so-called 'big four' – Viña Concha y Toro, Viña Santa Rita, Viña San Pedro and Viña Santa Carolina – account between them for some 80 percent of all the national brands sold on the domestic market. A group of intermediate size, including Errázuriz/Caliterra, Undurraga, Cánepa and Manquehue, supply most of the rest, leaving only a small share of the internal market to the smaller wineries, which are now turning to exports.

Exports of wines as a whole have grown by some 800 percent and of bottled wines by 1,000 percent over the period 1984–92, and are playing an increasingly important part in the booming Chilean economy, which itself grew by an astonishing 10 percent during 1992–93. The increase is due to the striking improvements in the quality of the wine and good quality/cost ratio, as well as to efficient promotion. For this purpose the larger companies have banded together in the Asociación de Exportadores y Embotalledores, while the others, belonging to a 'No 2 Committee', are represented by the government export agency, PROCHILE.

Until the mid-1980s the lion's share of exports was to the other countries of Latin America, with some going to the USA and Canada and a little to Europe. I remember that the first Chilean wine I tasted (from Cousiño Macul and Concha y Toro) in the mid-1960s was at the Hispanic Council in London and had been supplied by the Nitrate Corporation of Chile. Hugh Johnson in our *Chilean Wines* relates how he, too, in 1969, was much impressed by a Chilean bottle from Cánepa which came his way. He later ordered no less than a hogshead from the sole importer at the time, the now defunct Woolley, Duval and Beaufoys.

In a paper presented to the OIV Conference in San Francisco in August 1993, Professor Alejandro Hernández of the Catholic University in Santiago and Douglas Murray of Discover Wine traced subsequent developments. From 1985 Latin American markets stabilized, while there was rapid growth in the USA and Canada, but, for political reasons, it was not until General Pinochet stepped down that accelerated growth began in Europe, led by the UK. It is envisaged that in the future Europe will become the largest market.

There is an interesting sidelight in this paper on the different strategies pursued by the two largest Chilean wine firms in breaking into the American market:

> Viña Concha y Toro, who can be considered the true pioneers in the USA market, devised a simple but very effective campaign: keep prices reasonable at whatever cost. They must have sold at cost or at a loss for long periods, at times when the US dollar/peso exchange rate was very unfavourable and just about all other wineries reduced their

exports to a minimum. In sticking to their guns, Viña Concha y Toro was the winery in the best position to take off quickly in the USA when conditions improved.

Viña Santa Rita followed a different strategy. Firmly believing that the price niche was a vulnerable one, their path was to offer premium wines at higher price and to support their quality claims with a string of gold and silver medals in the best International Competitions and by topping the 'Gault Millau' list one year. This strategy helped Viña Santa Rita establish themselves as quality wines and, needless to say, their success at competitions directed great attention to Chilean wines in general and thus helped all wineries.

Total production of wine in 1992 was 152,028,356 litres, of which 56,401,794 litres were exported in bottle and 16,375,659 litres in bulk. Forty percent of exports went to Latin America, 28 percent to the USA, 11 percent to Canada and 19 percent to Europe, where the UK was by far the largest consumer. Viña Concha y Toro topped the list of exporters with some 1.3 million cases valued at US$25.5 million, followed by Viña Santa Rita with 393,000 cases sold for US$12.5 million, and Viña San Pedro with 548,000 cases and proceeds of US$11.9 million.

GLOSSARY OF WINE TERMS

WORDS USED ON WINE LABELS

antigua reserva mature wine of good quality, oak-aged for several years and aged further in bottle

brut dry, used only of sparkling wines

cepaje, cepaje noble Vine variety, noble vine variety

champaña sparkling wine. This may be made either by the champagne method or in *cuves closes.*

cosecha vintage, eg *cosecha* 1990

elaborado por produced by

embotellado en origen bottled at the winery

embotellado por bottled by

envasado por bottled by

fundada en founded in

grado, grado alcohólico alcohol content. 12° means that the wine contains 12 percent by volume of alcohol

gran vino wine of good quality, probably three to four years old

reserva, gran reserva very elastic terms in Chile, indicating simply that the wine is of good quality and has been aged for a time in wood and bottle

sirvase frío serve cold

viña a wine firm, eg Viña Santa Carolina

viñedo, viñedos proprios vineyard, grown in the company's own vineyards (estate-grown)

vino wine

    blanco white

    clarete light red

    dulce sweet

    rosado rosé

    tinto red

MISCELLANEOUS

agua water

agua de soda soda water

agua mineral mineral water

    con gas sparkling

    sin gas still

aguardiente grape spirit, brandy

arrope a syrup made by evaporating down must

barrica a small oak cask (usually of 225 litres) for maturing wine

bodega a winery

bomba a pump

brazo one of the main branches of a vine

en cabeza traditional system of growing wines low and 'goblet-shaped' (Spanish *en vaso*)

caña glass of wine

caramayola a flagon similar in shape to the German *bocksbeutel*

catador a wine taster

cepa a vine stock

cepaje *encépagement* – the blend of grape varieties used in making a wine

chicha young, partially fermented wine, popular in country districts

cooperativa a cooperative

cosechero owner of a vineyard, used of small independent producers

crema liqueur

    de cacao cocoa-based

    de café coffee-based

    de menta crème de menthe

    de naranja curaçao

cuba a fermentation vat

degustación tasting

Denominación de Origen, DO the demarcation of a wine or spirit from an officially recognized region. The term corresponds to the French Appellation d'Origine Contrôlée.

enología, enólogo oenology, oenologist

etiqueta a label

fudre a large barrel for maturing wine

fundo small country property

gerente the manager of a winery

a granel in bulk

grano the berry of a grape

hectárea a hectare of 2.471 acres

hectolitro a hectolitre of 22 gallons

hollejo grape-skin

ingeniero agrónomo an agronomist

injerto a graft

licor liqueur, spirit

levadura a yeast

mistela sweet must in which fermentation has been arrested by the addition of alcohol

mosto must, the juice extracted from the grapes prior to fermentation

orujo the skins and grape pips

pajarete a sweet, fortified wine

pipeño unfiltered wine which contains the by-products of fermentation

pisco the colourless brandy made from Moscatel grapes produced on a large scale in Chile

poda pruning

prensa a wine press

raulí the South American beech, formerly much used for making barrels and vats

reglamento the statutory rules for the making of wines and spirits covered by a Denominación de Origen

riego irrigation, regularly practised in the Central Valley

roble oak

sarmiento a vine shoot

socio member of a cooperative winery

uva a grape

    de mesa table, dessert grape

vasija a barrel (of any size) used for maturing wine

vendimia the wine harvest

vid a vine

viña a vineyard, also a wine company, eg Viña Undurraga

viñedo vineyard

vino wine (see also page 52)

    asoleado wine made from sunned grapes

    del año wine from the last harvest

viticultor a wine-grower

viticultura the cultivation of vines for winemaking

zona de secano an unirrigated wine area

ORDERING WINES AND DRINKS

May I see the wine list?	**La carta de vinos, por favor**
I should like a bottle/ half-bottle of . . . /a carafe/ half-carafe of house wine	**Por favor traiga una botella/ media botella de . . ./una jarra/ media jarra de vino de la casa**
Where does your house wine come from?	**¿De donde es el vino de la casa?**
Can you recommend a good local wine?	**¿Puede usted recomendar un vino bueno de la región?**
Yes, I should like a bottle	**Si, me gustaría una botella**

I should like to drink a red/ dry white/sweet white wine	Me gustaría beber un vino tinto/vino blanco seco/ vino blanco dulce
Can you please chill the wine?	¿Por favor puede usted enfriar el vino?
The waiter will probably begin by asking if you would like an aperitif	¿Quieren ustedes un apéritivo?
Depending on whether you would like one or not, the answer is: Yes, I should like a . . . and the lady/ my friend a . . .	Si, por favor, un . . . para mi y un . . . para la señora/el señor
No, thank you	No gracias
After you have ordered the wine, he will ask you whether, as is usual in Chile you want mineral water	¿Quieren ustedes agua mineral?
Yes, I should like a bottle/half-bottle of still/sparkling	Si, por favor. Me gustaría una botella/media botella sin gas/con gas
At the end of the meal the waiter will ask you if you want coffee	¿Quieren tomar café?
Yes, I/we should like black coffee/ white coffee/coffee with a little milk	Si, por favor, me/nos gustaría café solo/café con leche/café cortado
Except in expensive restaurants, if you want brandy or a liqueur at the table, you should ask for it: I/we should like a brandy/liqueur. What sorts do you have?	Me/nos gustaría tomar un aguardiente/licor. ¿Qué marcas tienen?
And to ask for the bill	La cuenta, por favor

THE WINERIES
AND THEIR WINES

HOW TO READ AN ENTRY

Entries are generally of two types: those describing a region, and those relating to individual producers (*viñas*) and their wines. The producers are listed under the five regions demarcated by the Chilean Ministry of Agriculture and recognized by the EC.

The regions are further divided into subregions, with whose names the wines are often labelled. (A full list of the subregions according to region can be found on page 32.) Some of the large concerns possess vineyards and vinification plants in several regions and are accordingly entered more than once. The top line of each entry referring to producers generally gives the following information:

1   The full name of the producer;
2   Whether the wine is bottled with a Denominación de Origen (DO). See Wine Law, pages 176–8;
3   The types of wine made by the producer, for example red, rosé, white, sparkling, in abbreviated form (see Key to Symbols, opposite).

Stars have not been used as most of the wineries make a range of wines of differing quality. Moreover, detailed tasting notes are provided for most of the wines, and these act as a much more precise guide as to what may be expected.

Vintages are specified only in the tasting notes. In general, the climate is so benign and so consistent, with months of unbroken sunshine in summer, that there is little to choose between one year and another. I have yet to see a vintage list in any Chilean publication.

Next, the address and telephone number of the producer are provided, and in the case of the larger firms those of the head office in Santiago. This information will be needed when arranging visits to the wineries (see pages 15–16). When making local calls, omit the area code given in brackets.

A NOTE ON THE TASTING NOTES

The wines were tasted by myself and Maite Manjón, mostly during visits to the wineries in March 1993. Other tastings are indicated by date. Much as we like fruity wines, we are not of the 'fruit, nothing but fruit and more fruit' school (and especially fruit described in winespeak as 'blackcurranty', 'banana-y', 'kiwi-y', 'toffee-y' and so on). Our response to this is like that of the Parisian restaurateur in *Ninotchka* who, reacting to Garbo's demand for raw beef and raw carrots, exclaims: 'But, Madame, this is a restaurant, not a meadow.' And it seems to us that there is more to be gained from Michael Broadbent's imaginative likening of a blockbusting but closed wine to a laden jumbo jet labouring to take off than from comparisons ranging, in the same breath, from Dundee cake to kippers, petrol or orange blossom. We hope, at any rate, that these straightforward notes will be helpful.

KEY TO SYMBOLS

DO	Denominación de Origen	**dr**	dry
r	red	**sw**	sweet
p	rosé	**res**	*reserva*
w	white	**g**	*generoso* (fortified wine)
sp	sparkling	**( )**	denotes less important wine

Cross-references in the tasting notes to wineries which are also discussed under their own, separate entry are shown in small capital letters.

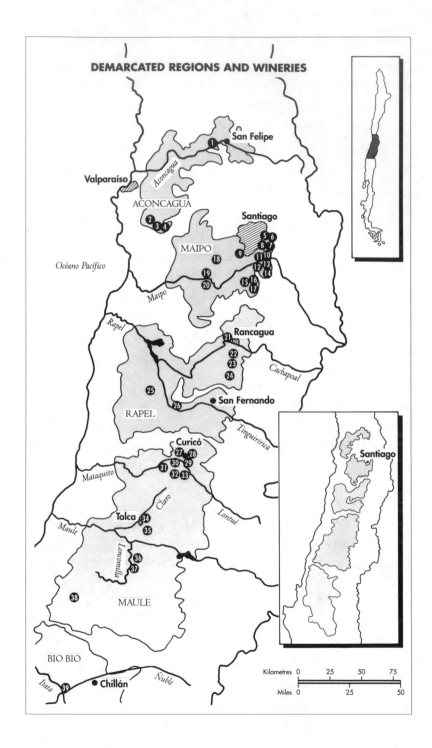

DEMARCATED REGIONS AND WINERIES

Demarcated Regions and Wineries Key		
❶ Errázuriz	⓭ Domaine Rabat	㉗ Discover Wine
❷ Santa Emiliana	⓮ Concha y Toro	㉘ Cooperativa Curicó
❸ Casablanca	⓯ Santa Rita	㉙ Torres
❹ Villard Fine Wines	⓰ Carmen	㉚ Caliterra
❺ Mitjans	⓱ Portal del Alto	㉛ Valdivieso
❻ Manquehue	⓲ Undurraga	㉜ San Pedro
❼ Aquitania	⓳ Santa Ema	㉝ Echeverría
❽ Cousiño Macul	⓴ Santa Inés	㉞ Cooperativa Talca
❾ Cánepa	㉑ Santa Mónica	㉟ Domaine Oriental
❿ Tarapacá Ex-Zavala	㉒ Porta	㊱ Carta Vieja
⓫ Santa Carolina	㉓ Santa Amalia	㊲ Segu Ollé
⓬ Santa Adela	㉔ Torreón de Paredes	㊳ Cooperativa Cauquenes
	㉕ Los Vascos	
	㉖ Bisquertt	㊴ Itata

ACONCAGUA

Aconcagua is the only region making beverage wines to be located north of Santiago, some 200 kilometres (120 miles) away. The wide valley opens out towards the Pacific north of the town of Valparaíso and is watered by the Aconcagua flowing down from the highest peaks of the Andes. The mildly alkaline and permeable soils and an arid Mediterranean climate, tempered by cooling sea breezes, are well suited for viticulture, but the area as a whole is a large-scale producer of table grapes. There are only two subregions, Panquehue and Casablanca which make wines, albeit extremely good ones.

Casablanca DO w dr (r)

This fast-developing subregion lies some 30 kilometres (20 miles) southeast of Valparaíso in the hilly country of the Casablanca Valley. The area has poor soils and was formerly given over to 'survival farming'. Its potential for viticulture was first recognized by the agricultural engineer Pablo Morande, who noticed ecological and climatic similarities to Napa and Sonoma counties in California, and planted an experimental 20 hectares with Chardonnay, Riesling and Sauvignon Blanc in 1982. The nearness of the cold Humboldt Current and the prevalence of cooling Pacific breezes result in very marked differences between daytime and night-time temperatures. As a result the vines flower a week after those of Maipo to the south and the grapes, harvested a month later, are high in both sugar and acid.

Morande's experiment proved so successful that approximately 950 hectares have now been planted in the valley, mainly with Chardonnay. The major concerns of CONCHA Y TORO, SANTA CAROLINA, SANTA EMILIANA and SANTA RITA have all begun planting on a significant scale, as also specialist producers such as VILLARD FINE WINES. The largest project is that of the California-based FRANCISCAN VINEYARDS, which has purchased 3,500 hectares in the area.

'Casablanca' DO w dr (r)

Brand name for the excellent wines from VIÑA CASABLANCA, of two types: those from the Casablanca Valley itself and the White Label wines from other regions.

Casablanca Ltda, Viña DO w dr (r)

Rodrigo de Araya 1431, Santiago, Tel (2) 238 0390

Viña Casablanca is an associate company of VIÑA SANTA CAROLINA, recently formed to develop the winery's vineyards in the new Casablanca subregion. The existing 50 hectares of the Santa Isabel estate are near the sea and sheltered by carob trees. Planted mainly with drip-fed Chardonnay and Sauvignon Blanc, they are being extended and a new winery is being constructed; at the moment, the wines are vinified by Santa Carolina. Casablanca's oenologist is the brilliant young Ignacio Recabarren, one of the 'Young Turks' with wide experience of winemaking in France, California, Australia and New Zealand.

Viña Casablanca was one of the few concerns to make small amounts of the 1992 wine from the valley, which was badly affected by untimely frosts the previous spring. Further amounts of the 1992 vintage were made with grapes from the Maipo, Rapel and Maule regions.

White Wines

'Casablanca' Sauvignon Blanc 1993 (tasted July 1993)
From the Casablanca Valley. Pale straw. Marvellously flowery nose and luscious taste of tropical fruit rather than of gooseberries or flowering currant. Long peachy finish.

'Casablanca' Sauvignon Blanc 1992
From the Santa Isabel estate in the Casablanca Valley. Picked late in April. 50 percent barrel fermented in French oak barriques and 50 percent in stainless steel. 12° alcohol. Pale straw. Complex floral and herbal nose. Appley, almost Riesling flavour. A touch of quince. Slightly reminiscent of a Spanish Albariño. Long finish. Delicate and very nice.

'Casablanca' White Label 1993 (tasted June 1993)
From the Lontué Valley (Maule). Pale lemon. Remarkably fresh nose and taste of tropical fruit – pineapple, melon, peaches. Long peachy finish. Delicious.

'Casablanca' White Label Sauvignon Blanc 1992
From the Lontué Valley (Maule). This blend was made specially by Ignacio Recabarren in consultation with Manuel Moreno and Carlos Read for shipment by Moreno Wines, London. Fermented in stainless steel. Lemon yellow. Melon nose. Clean and refreshing with an assortment of tropical fruit culled from Carmen Miranda's cornucopia.

'Casablanca' Chardonnay 1992
From the Santa Isabel estate in the Casablanca Valley. 100 percent fermented in French oak barriques with 100 percent malolactic. 12.9° alcohol. Complex oaky Chardonnay nose. Very strong buttery Chardonnay in the mouth. The wine is full-bodied and has a long finish. Very good.

'Casablanca' Gewürztraminer 1992 (tasted July 1993)

From the Santa Isabel estate in the Casablanca Valley. 100 percent Gewürz-traminer fermented in stainless steel. Lemon colour. Honeyed, fragrant nose. Soft and refreshing with lemon verbena taste, but a bit bland. When tasted the next day the wine had developed a strong peachy nose and taste.

Red Wines

'Casablanca' White Label Cabernet Sauvignon Reserva 1991

From the Maipo Valley. Kept on the skins for two and a half weeks. 100 percent aged in French oak barriques. Ruby. Nicely balanced fruit and oak on the nose. Round and soft with plenty of ripe blackcurrant fruit. Long finish. An excellent claret-like wine.

'Casablanca' Cabernet Sauvignon 1990

From the Miraflores estate, San Fernando Valley (Rapel). Dark cherry. Fruity Cabernet nose. Nice blend of oak and full berry fruit. Long finish. Excellent.

'Don Maximiano'

This red special reserve from ERRAZURIZ PANQUEHUE is made from Cabernet Sauvignon, sometimes with the addition of a little Cabernet Franc and Merlot, and aged for 20–24 months in oak.

Errázuriz Panquehue SA, Viña DO r w dr res

Av Nueva Costanera 3759, Santiago, Tel (2) 242 2985

Don Maximiano Errázuriz Valdivieso once said that: 'Grape vines should be carefully tended and treated like a work of art, since their lifespan runs parallel to that of man . . . A vine should be cared for and properly pruned and trained so that its branches bear the highest quality fruit.'

Like other Chilean aristocrats of the period, Don Maximiano, who founded Errázuriz in 1870, obtained and planted vine stocks from France, but he was alone in starting a vineyard well to the north of Santiago in the

Aconcagua Valley near the town of San Felipe; it was generally predicted that the venture would fail. To the contrary, the soils and climate proved well suited to viticulture, so much so that his son, Rafael Errázuriz Urmeneta, extended the plantations to 1,000 hectares, thus creating the single largest vineyard in the world at the time. The vineyard area in the Aconcagua Valley has since declined, although the vine stock has survived and is used for making the bodega's premium 'Don Maximiano'. Errázuriz has also bought 156 hectares in Sagrada Familia in the DO Maule, from which it obtains the grapes for its Chardonnay, Sauvignon Blanc and Merlot.

In 1983 the firm was taken over by the Chadwick family, who first settled in Chile in 1839. The mother of Alfonso Chadwick, now president of the company, was an Errázuriz, so the family tradition remains unbroken. Under the dynamic management of Alfonso and his son Eduardo there has been extensive modernization. The beautiful old winery, with its tiled roof and deep underground cellars, constructed by French architects, has been completely re-equipped with stainless steel tanks for fermenting the wine and some 4,000 new 225-litre casks of Allier, Nevers and American oak.

In 1988 Errázuriz embarked on an ambitious new project when it joined forces with the well-known FRANCISCAN VINEYARDS of California to launch VIÑA CALITERRA, with vineyards in Curicó and Maipo. Errázuriz subsequently bought out Franciscan Vineyards, and Caliterra is now 100 percent Chilean owned. Both concerns export most of their wines, particularly to the UK. Tasting notes for the Caliterra wines are separately listed under Maule.

White Wines

Sauvignon Blanc 1992
From the firm's Maule Valley estate. 12° alcohol. Pale straw. Extremely aromatic with overtones of flowering currant and kiwi. Light and luscious with a touch of gooseberry and good acidity.

Sauvignon Blanc Reserva 1992
Made with grapes from 50-year-old vines in the Maule Valley. 25 percent of the must was fermented in new American oak casks. 12.3° alcohol.

Pale lemon. Less pronounced bouquet and fruit with hint of oak. Somewhat bland and a bit peppery at the finish.

Chardonnay 1993 (tasted January 1994)

From the Maule Valley. Half fermented in French oak and half in stainless steel, then mixed with further ageing in oak. 13° alcohol. Pale straw. Delicious apple and gooseberry nose with a little oak. Light Chardonnay and green fruit in middle. Not buttery. Oaky finish. Nice.

Chardonnay 1992

13° alcohol. Pale lemon. Subdued Chardonnay nose. Marked Chardonnay flavour, but uncomplicated and rather bland.

Chardonnay Reserva 1992

Nose and flavour not as developed as with the 1991, but a delicate wine and very clean.

Chardonnay Reserva 1991

Made with grapes grown in the Maule Valley. Barrel fermented in new French oak. 13° alcohol. Lemon yellow. Pronounced oaky Chardonnay nose; apple and pineapple flavours with overtones of buttery oak. Long finish. Nice.

Red Wines

Merlot 1991

Made with grapes from the firm's estate in the Maule Valley. 100 percent Merlot. 12° alcohol. Dark, plummy red. Very fruity damson nose. Sweet, ripe, damson fruit. Good finish. Wonderful. (The 1992 vintage was very similar, but more tannic.)

'Don Maximiano' 1990

100 percent Cabernet Sauvignon from the Aconcagua Valley. Matured for 20–24 months in new oak casks. 12.7° alcohol. Don Maximiano is a juicy, full-bodied wine with rich blackcurrant and oak flavours, described by some (Jane MacQuitty) as 'uncomplicated' and by others (Danish Neils Ole Madsen) as 'of similar calibre to Château Latour at one sixth the price.' This sample had perhaps not been opened in time to breathe; it was somewhat tannic and the fruit seemed masked by the oak.

Franciscan Vineyards

The most ambitious project in the Casablanca Valley has been mounted by Franciscan Vineyards of California at Viña El Cabilde de Casablanca, of which 50 percent belongs to the well-known Chilean winemaker Agustín Huneeus, who at one time headed the country's largest wine concern, CONCHA Y TORO.

The 3,500-hectare property lies to the east of the Casablanca Valley, with temperatures 2–3°C (3.5–6.5°F) higher than in the central and western parts. At present 200 of the 500 hectares suitable for growing grapes are being planted with Chardonnay; further plantings of the red Merlot and Sangiovese will follow. For the time being the grapes will be sold to other producers, but plans are afoot for building a winery making only estate-bottled wines.

Panquehue DO r

Subregion to the east of Aconcagua Valley in the foothills of the Andes between the towns of Llay-Llay and San Felipe, famous for VIÑA ERRAZURIZ PANQUEHUE.

Santa Carolina SA, Viña DO w dr

Rodrigo de Araya 1431, Santiago, Tel (2) 238 0307

VIÑA SANTA CAROLINA has handed over the 50 hectares of its Santa Isabel estate to a newly formed associate company, VIÑA CASABLANCA.

Santa Emiliana SA, Bodegas y Viñedos DO w d

Fernando Lazcano 1220, Santiago, Tel (2) 555 5670

Santa Emiliana, with a winery in the town of Maipo and extensive vineyards in the Rapel Region, has a holding of 160 hectares in the Casablanca Valley. Because of severe frosts, no wine from the Casablanca vineyards was made in 1992, and the 1992 Santa Emiliana Sauvignon Blanc was made with grapes from Rancagua and Rengo.

Santa Rita Ltda, Viña DO w dr (r)

Gertrudis Echenique 49, Santiago, Tel (2) 228 9166

Like other major wine firms, Santa Rita is alive to the potential of Casablanca and present and future plantings amount to 90 hectares of Chardonnay, 14 hectares of Sauvignon Blanc and 10 hectares of Merlot.

Villard Fine Wines DO w dr r

Miravalle 9416, Las Condes, Santiago 10, Tel (2) 220 2120

Thierry Villard was born in Paris but speaks with an Australian accent, and indeed spent many years in Australia, first marketing French wines and then contributing to the modernization of the Australian wine industry and the astonishing success of that country's wines overseas. With all the enterprise of his adopted compatriots, he then decided he wanted to make his own wines. Being married to a Chilean and aware of the quality of Chilean wines, he settled in the country in 1989, setting up Villard Fine Wines with the cooperation of local producers in the Casablanca Valley. The company now owns 50 hectares, together with vineyards in the Central Valley for the production of red wines. Villard is also associated with SANTA EMILIANA and is therefore able to make use of Emiliana's vinification plant and to draw on the services of its oenologist, although Villard is currently constructing his own winery.

Thierry Villard is a perfectionist and goes to great pains to achieve the best possible quality. For example, the grapes are picked in the cool of the early morning or after sunset, and the casks are imported from Tonnellerie Ludaunnaise, one of the most recondite of French cooperages. In view of his high standards and because of severe frost damage, Villard made no wine from the Casablanca subregion in 1992.

White Wines

Sauvignon Blanc 1993 (tasted January 1994)

From Casablanca Valley. 13° alcohol. Pale straw. Attractive perfumed nose with hint of cinnamon, but also a little sulphur. Lichees and melon in the middle, but the end is a bit tame. The wine gathers intensity with airing, but the slight sulphur persists.

Sauvignon Blanc 1992

From Lontué (Maule). Pale straw. Subdued nose. Round and refreshing. Good acidity and finish.

Chardonnay 1992

From Lontué (Maule). Six to eight hours' skin contact. Four days' fermentation in stainless steel at 15°C (59°F), then 60 percent of wine transferred to barriques and left on lees for eight months. Pronounced oaky Chardonnay nose. Intense buttery flavour. Good finish.

Chardonnay 1991

From Lontué (Maule). 60 percent aged in French oak barriques and left on lees for eight months. Pale yellow. Not much nose, but attractive, rather smoky oak in the middle with good acidity.

Red Wine

Cabernet Sauvignon 1990

From Chimbarongo (Rapel). Fermented at 26–28°C (79–82°F) for a week, left on lees for two weeks, matured in French oak barriques for nine months, then kept in epoxy-lined tanks and bottled after two years. Dark ruby. Good Cabernet nose, intense berry fruit and long finish.

MAIPO

The region of Maipo lies mainly in the Metropolitan Region to the west and south of Santiago, and centres on the Maipo River as it flows from the Andes into the Pacific at San Antonio. It is divided into six subregions: Santiago, Buin, Isla de Maipo, Llano de Maipo, Pirque and Santa Ana. It is classed as semi-arid with an annual average of 300 millimetres of rain, and the vineyards, like most of those in the Central Valley, are irrigated with water from the Andes. Although Maipo is the most famous Chilean wine region, 12,945 hectares are planted with table grapes as against 2,479 hectares with those for making wine, rather more red than white. This was the heartland where the aristocratic mine-owners and agriculturalists of the late 19th century began the regeneration of the Chilean wine industry with vine stocks brought from France and Germany, and it is still home to many of the most prestigious names in the industry: CONCHA Y TORO, COUSIÑO MACUL, SANTA CAROLINA, SANTA RITA and UNDURRAGA among others.

'120' DO r w dr

These well-known red and white wines from SANTA RITA take their name from the famous occasion after the defeat of Bernardo O'Higgins by the Spaniards at the Battle of Rancagua in 1814 during the War of Independence, when he and 120 followers took refuge at Santa Rita. The cellar in which they were reputedly hidden has recently been reconstructed as a museum.

'Antiguas Reservas' DO r res

This classic from COUSIÑO MACUL is perhaps the most famous of the Chilean red *reservas*. Made from Cabernet Sauvignon grown on slopes with maximum sun exposure, it was formerly aged for three years in cask and two in bottle to meet the Chilean taste for old, oaky wines. Since the bodega invested in new American oak, maturation in cask has been reduced to eight months, resulting in fruitier and fresher wines appealing more to the international taste (see Cousiño Macul and tasting notes on the 1979 and 1988 vintages).

Aquitania Ltda, Sociedad Agrícola DO r (w dr)

A new concern initiated by Bruno Prats of Cos d'Estournel and Paul Pontallier of Château Margaux in partnership with a Chilean oenologist. Some 25 hectares in the Andean foothills overlooking Santiago have been planted with Cabernet Sauvignon, and arrangements have been made to buy fruit from neighbouring producers. From 1993, the aim is to produce wines comparable in quality with those made by the partners in Bordeaux.

Buin

Buin is a subregion of Maipo and is named after the town lying to the east of the region between the rivers Maipo and Cachapoal in the foothills of the Andes. Its best-known wineries are SANTA RITA and PORTAL DEL ALTO.

Cánepa y Cía Ltda, Viña José DO w dr r res

Luis Tayber Ojeda 236, 6th Floor, Santiago, Tel (2) 233 1311

José Cánepa Vacarezza, whose recent death was a loss to the entire Chilean wine industry, arrived in Valparaíso in 1914 from his native Italy at the tender age of 15. After spending 15 years in the wine trade with relatives, the young Cánepa set up a distributing business before setting out to fulfil a dream of making his own wines. His first move was to buy land in the so-called Isla de Maipo, then a stony, arid enclave where the Maipo River bends back on itself. Using an ingenious system of dams, Cánepa enriched the soil with sediment from the river to create a flourishing vineyard. He later acquired properties further south in the Maule Region, at Peteroa in Sagrada Familia and at the Hacienda San Jorge near Curicó. From these beginnings, he built up vineyards of some 400 hectares planted with the best French stock.

In 1980 Don José took an equally important step by constructing the most modern winery in South America, at Maipu, equipping it with temperature-controlled stainless steel tanks, made in California and heavily ribbed to withstand earthquakes. Their current capacity is 6.5 million litres, in addition to 1.2 million litres for fermentation and storage in wood. Like all the wineries, Cánepa has invested heavily in new oak casks from France and the USA; and the rest of the equipment – crushers, presses, vacuum filters, refrigeration plant and bottling line – is state-of-the-art and brought from the ends of the earth.

Cánepa is also a major producer and exporter of fruit, with over 1,000 hectares of orchards growing apples, oranges and lemons, avocados, peaches, nuts, and olives for making olive oil.

For all his commercial success, Don José was intensely humane, building solid houses for his workers and schools for their children. To encourage attendance, each child was given a large loaf of bread to take home, and the tradition of 'Cánepa Bread' still survives.

There are two main families of wine: the young 'Novísimo' varietals fermented at low temperature in stainless steel to conserve the maximum of fruit, and the more complex 'Finísimo' wines, matured in oak. 80 percent of the annual production of some 6 million bottles is exported to more than 20 countries.

White Wines

Sauvignon Blanc 1993 (tasted December 1993)
Straw-coloured with greenish cast. Very fruity flowering currant nose. A little smoky. Fresh flowering currant taste. Good acidity and finish.
'Novísimo' Sauvignon Blanc 1992
12.5° alcohol. Bright pale straw. Floral nose. Light and lively with taste of kiwi, but lacking somewhat in acidity. Rather bland and lacks bite with food.
Sémillon 1993 tank sample (tasted December 1993)
Pale straw. Fragrant flowery and honeyed nose. Very slight *pétillance*. Delicate pineapple taste, gooseberry at end. Good acidity and finish. Very nice.

'Clasico' Sémillon 1992

From Isla de Maipo. 13° alcohol. Pale straw. Very fragrant floral nose. Clean, fresh and fragrant with minty taste and long finish. A first-rate Sémillon.

Chardonnay 1993 (tasted December 1993)

Fermented 100 percent in stainless steel. Pale yellow with peachy nose. Very fresh and tastes of peaches and gooseberries. Round, buttery and full-bodied with good acidity.

'Novísimo' Chardonnay 1991

13° alcohol. Lemon yellow. Matured in French oak for six months and one year in bottle. Nice Chardonnay nose. Good buttery flavour with touch of oak. Satisfactory finish. Very pleasant.

Chardonnay 'Reserva' 1993 (tasted January 1994)

Pale straw. Lovely fragrant nose with a touch of oak. Clean as a whistle. Chardonnay, lichees and papaya in middle. Good acidity and finish. Beautiful.

Experimental Chardonnay 1992

Fermented in 225-litre barriques. Fragrant, perfumed nose. Fresh and very intense flavour with touch of wood. Good finish, very promising.

Red Wines

'Novísimo' Cabernet Sauvignon 1992

Stainless steel only. Dark cherry. Lively blackcurrant nose. Intensely alive and fruity. Meaty and long. Beautiful young wine.

Experimental Cabernet Sauvignon-Merlot 1991

One year in stainless steel and one in bottle. Dark ruby. Smooth and bursting with plummy fruit, soft tannin. Good finish.

Cabernet Sauvignon 1990

One year in American oak, some new and some older, then blended. Dark cherry. Nice Cabernet nose with refined vanilla oak. Soft fruit. Herbal and spicy. Very good balance.

Cabernet Sauvignon Special Reserva 1990

One year in new American oak, 18 months in bottle. Dark ruby. Well balanced, herbal and spicy with masses of fruit. More tannic than the others at end.

Carmen, Viña DO r w dr res

Gertrudis Echenique 49, Santiago, Tel (2) 246 2895

Founded in 1850 by Don Cristián Lanz, this is one of the oldest Chilean wine companies. It was later taken over by VIÑA CANEPA and acquired by Don Ricardo Claro of VIÑA SANTA RITA in 1988. It now possesses extensive vineyards in the Maipo, Rapel and Maule valleys; and a state-of-the-art winery in Alto Jahuel near Buin in the Maipo Valley with a 3.5 million-litre capacity began operations in 1993. Its talented oenologist is Alvaro Espinoza Durán, who studied at Bordeaux University and worked at Château Margaux and Moët & Chandon, before returning to Chile to work first with DOMAINE ORIENTAL, coming to Viña Carmen in 1992. At the Bordeaux VINEXPO in 1993, Carmen won gold, silver and bronze medals for its Chardonnay 1993, Cabernet Sauvignon 1990 and Sauvignon Blanc 1993, respectively.

White Wines

Sauvignon Blanc 1993 (tasted June 1993)
From the Maule Valley. Unfiltered. 13.2° alcohol. Pale lemon. Pineapple and tropical fruit in nose. Clean, light and very grapey with taste of melons and tropical fruit. Good honeyed finish.

Sauvignon Blanc Reserve 1993 (tasted June 1993)
From the Maule Valley. 13.2° alcohol. Pale straw. Fruity nose and taste – quince and a touch of mint and lichees. Good acidity and finish.

Chardonnay 1993 (tasted June 1993)
From the Maipo Valley. Lemon yellow. 13.3° alcohol. Very fruity and fragrant Chardonnay nose. Clean with good body and taste of quince and bananas. Good acidity and long finish. Very nice.

Red Wines

Merlot 1991 (tasted June 1993)
From the Rapel Valley. 12.3° alcohol. Dark cherry. Plummy nose and taste. A bit sharp.

Cabernet Sauvignon 1990 (tasted July 1993)

From the Maipo Valley. 12.5° alcohol. Dark cherry red. Closed nose. Some fruit, but a bit sharp and very dry.

Cabernet Sauvignon Reserve 1990 (tasted June 1993)

From the Maipo Valley. 12.5° alcohol. Very dark cherry. Fruity nose with touch of oak. Round, soft and juicy with blackberry fruit, but lacking complexity. Delicate wood. Good finish. Opens out and becomes much softer and more mellow with half an hour's airing.

'Casillero del Diablo' DO w dr r res

One of the best-known red wines from CONCHA Y TORO. It was a special favourite of the bodega's founder, Don Melchor de Santiago Concha who, to frighten off intruders, put it about that the corner of the cellars where he kept his private reserve was haunted by the devil. Concha y Toro later founded a wine fraternity by the same name.

Concha y Toro SA, Viña DO w dr & sw r res
Fernando Lazcano 1220, Santiago, Tel (2) 556 7882

Concha y Toro is the largest Chilean wine company in terms of both domestic sales and exports. The story begins when Don Ramón Subercaseaux, a wealthy mine-owner of French origin, bought the 5,920-hectare estate of Pirque south of the Maipo River. The tract was flat, dry and covered with bushes, but by diverting a supply of water from the river he was able to turn it into good agricultural land. He employed a French oenologist, a M Bachelet, to plant a vineyard, and built a bodega and houses for his workers.

Don Ramón's daughter, Doña Emiliana, married a brilliant young entrepreneur, Don Melchor de Santiago Concha, a descendant of the first Marqués de Casa Concha, who came to Chile in 1717 as a representative of the Viceroyalty of Peru. The firm of Concha y Toro was established in 1883 when Don Melchor obtained more French vine stock and, on the advice of his talented French oenologist, M de Labouchère, bought a further large estate at Peumo near Rancagua.

The business grew apace after Don Melchor's death in 1892 and because of its size, and problems concerning the inheritance, Don Melchor's grand-daughters (there were no grandsons) decided in 1923 to launch it as a public company. Since then the firm has further expanded, and has prospered under efficient and dynamic management. Control now lies with Don Eduardo Guilisaste Tagle, president since 1971, and Don Alfonso Larraín Santa María, general manager and managing director. The chief oenologist, Sr Goetz von Gersdorff, came to the company from Germany 25 years ago, bringing with him special expertise in making white wines.

Concha y Toro owns 1,207 hectares of vineyards in current production:

Maipo Region	Puente Alto	214 ha
	Santa Isabel	81 ha
	Pirque	43 ha
Rapel Region	Peumo	383 ha
	Rucahue	84 ha
Maule Region	Lourdes	287 ha
	Rauco	115 ha

A further 497 hectares were planted in 1993. The grape varieties include a preponderance of Cabernet Sauvignon, substantial amounts of Merlot, Sémillon and Riesling, together with Malbec, Sauvignon Blanc, Chardonnay, Verdot, Gewürztraminer and Chenin Blanc.

There are three vinification plants: at Puente Alto (Maipo), Peumo (Rapel) and Lontué (Maule), and cellars for maturing the wine at Pirque, Puente Alto, Peumo and Lontué. Total storage capacity is 54 million litres: 5.5 million litres in stainless steel tanks, 1.6 million litres in French and

American barriques, and the remainder in epoxy-coated cement tanks or in rauli vats and barrels. Concha y Toro dominates the domestic market with sales in 1992 of 31.5 million litres, or 21 percent of the total. The company also exported 20.6 million litres to 46 countries in 1992, of which 16.2 million litres were fine bottled wines.

The pride of Concha y Toro is the 'Don Melchor' special reserve, named after its founder and made only with Cabernet Sauvignon from the Pirque vineyards, of which Robert Parker wrote in *The Wine Advocate*: 'A terrific Cabernet Sauvignon . . . the best one I have drunk in Chile in a long time.' Other prestige labels are the 'Marqués de Casa Concha', available in Cabernet Sauvignon, Merlot and Chardonnay, and 'Casillero del Diablo', in Cabernet Sauvignon, Chardonnay and Sauvignon Blanc.

White Wines

Chardonnay 1992

No oak and no malolactic fermentation. 12° alcohol. Pale straw. Light Chardonnay nose. Clean, light gooseberry taste, but bland and lacks intensity.

'Casillero del Diablo' Chardonnay 1992

Blend of 50 percent fermented in American oak barriques and 50 percent in stainless steel. No malolactic. Pale lemon. More concentrated oaky nose and flavour. Good finish.

'Marqués de Casa Concha' Chardonnay 1992

100 percent fermented in French oak barriques and left on lees. 15 percent malolactic. Pale lemon. Chardonnay and light oak nose. More intense flavour and finish but still, like the others, rather light.

Red Wines

Cabernet Sauvignon 1991

Fermented in epoxy-coated cement tanks, transferred to rauli vats for malolactic, then returned to cement tanks. 11.7° alcohol. Dark cherry. Clean fruity nose. Mellow, with long legs denoting glycerine. Ripe and chocolatey, but a bit smooth and lacking tannin.

'Marqués de Casa Concha' Merlot 1991

From Peumo. Fermented in raulí vats, macerated with skins then transferred to French oak barriques, 50 percent new and 50 percent old. Dark cherry. Good plummy Merlot nose. Rich fruit with flavours of chocolate, blackberry and liquorice. Very soft, with long legs indicating glycerine. Good finish. Very pleasant.

'Casillero del Diablo' Cabernet Sauvignon 1990

From Pirque. 12.5° alcohol. Fermented in raulí. 80 percent aged in American oak barriques and 20 percent in epoxy-coated cement. Dark cherry. Luscious and soft with flavours of cherries and eucalyptus. Finish a bit bland. (From 1992 this wine will be fermented in stainless steel. In 1991 half was fermented in stainless steel and half in epoxy-coated cement, and Sr Goetz found no difference in quality.)

'Marqués de Casa Concha' Cabernet Sauvignon 1990

From Puente Alto. 13.5 percent alcohol. Very dark cherry. Eucalyptus nose. Ripe, full-bodied and oaky with marked eucalyptus flavour. A bit smooth – could do with a brisker, more tannic finish.

'Don Melchor' Cabernet Sauvignon 1989

From Puente Alto. 13.5° alcohol. Very dark cherry. Eucalyptus nose with a touch of cedar. A full-bodied, mellow and intense wine with flavours of blackcurrant, mint and spice. Long finish. A nice older wine which should last.

Cabernet Sauvignon 1984 (tasted November 1988)

As supplied to Waitrose, London. 12.5° alcohol. Very dark ruby. Spicy Cabernet nose. Lots of fruit in nose and mouth. Chocolate. Vigorous, beautiful, long finish. Marvellous value.

Cousiño Macul, Viña DO w dr r res

Av Quilin con Canal San Carlos, Santiago, Tel (2) 283 3000

The Cousiño family was one of the wealthiest and most influential in 19th-century Chile. The founder of its fortunes, Don Matías Cousiño Jorquera, owned silver mines, established a coal-mining industry at Lota in the south, was involved in the construction of the first railways in South America, and ran a shipping line to carry his coal and agricultural products to ports all along the coast from Lota to San Francisco. His son, Don Luis, married the heiress Isidora Goyenechea, and between them they extended the family's domain, founding Chile's leading newspaper, *El Mercurio*, hiring a French landscape architect to lay out the magnificent parks at Macul, Lota and in central Santiago, and constructing the great Cousiño Palace, furnished with tapestries, antiques and pictures brought from France.

The Macul vineyards, on the eastern fringes of the city of Santiago in the foothills of the Andes, are among the oldest in the country. They were first planted by Juan Jufré, a lieutenant of the Conquistador Pedro de Valdivia, in about 1554. The estate, acquired by Don Matías in 1856, was at the time planted with 5,000 of the local País vines. These were replaced with Cabernet Sauvignon, Sauvignon Blanc and Sémillon propagated from cuttings brought by Don Luis from France from the vineyards of Margaux and Pauillac in 1860. Before his sudden death in 1873, Don Luis engaged a firm of French architects to build cellars to the most advanced design of the time. They were excavated 5.5 metres (18 feet) underground, then lined with a double wall of brick and limestone, with an airspace between. The temperature varies by only 0.5°C (1°F) throughout the year. The wine library contains bottles of every vintage of Cousino Macul since 1927, and these are tasted and recorked every ten years.

Today the vineyard covers 267 hectares all planted with vines from existing stock. The most important plantings are 156 hectares of Cabernet Sauvignon, 29.7 hectares of Sémillon, 29.1 hectares of Sauvignon Blanc, 24 hectares of Riesling and 19 hectares of Chardonnay. All the wine is made from grapes grown on the Macul vineyard.

Cousiño Macul has always been rated as one of Chile's 'First Growths' but is not resting on its laurels. Under the direction of its chief oenologist and general manager, Jaime Ríos, planting density of the vines has been increased to improve the quality of the must. New crushers, pneumatic presses and stainless steel tanks have also been installed; and three years ago the winery ended a 130-year-old tradition when it began ageing the wine in new 200-litre oak barriques instead of large American oak barrels.

For decades the famous 'Antiguas Reservas', with its long years in oak, was the hallmark of Chilean taste in fine wines. Today the time spent maturing in cask is being limited in aid of fresher fruit and wood flavours in the red wines; and there is renewed emphasis on making clean and elegant young whites.

White Wines

Sauvignon Blanc 1992

12.8° alcohol. Pale lemon. Delicate floral nose. Clean, fresh with herbal flavours and a touch of flowering currant. Good finish.

Chardonnay 1992

Skin contact for four hours before fermentation in stainless steel. Pale lemon. Delicate Chardonnay nose. Luscious, light, with well-developed Chardonnay flavour and touch of lichees. Smoky finish.

Chardonnay Reserve 1990

Three months in American oak after fermentation in stainless steel. Pale lemon. Touch of vanilla in nose. Nice blend of gentle oak and fruit. Good finish. Attractive.

Red Wines

Merlot 1989

Made with selected clones of ten-year-old Merlot from the Macul vineyards. Fermented at 27–29°C (81–84°F) for five days. Malolactic fermentation in raulí vats, then matured in 225-litre barriques for four to seven months. Dark plum. Oak plus Merlot nose. Round and grapey with well-balanced fruit and oak and more than a touch of tannin.

Antiguas Reservas 1988

Eight months in American oak barriques. Deep ruby with orange rim. Intense Cabernet Sauvignon nose. Good blend of blackcurrant fruit and vanilla oak. Long finish. Very nice.

'Antiguas Reservas' *1979*

An example of the old style esteemed in Chile. Deep ruby. Raisiny, drying out and bitter with touch of phenol at end.

'Don Melchor' DO r res

The classiest of CONCHA Y TORO's Cabernet Sauvignons, named after its founder, Don Melchor de Santiago Concha, and much fancied by Robert Parker and *Wine Spectator*, which described it as 'the best Chilean red.'

Fundación Chile

Chile's leading agricultural research institute, funded jointly by the government and the American ITT Corporation. With its headquarters and extensive laboratories in Santiago, it carries out investigations in such fields as: forestry; marine resources; the growing, processing and packing of fruit and vegetables; and the environment generally. Its services and expertise are much in demand outside Chile, in South America at large and as far afield as Egypt.

The Fundación has planted 350 hectares of noble vines at Itata in the VIII Region and is constructing a modern winery, with the intention of restoring viticulture to an area where it was dying out. With undertakings such as this, the institute's policy is to sell the concern once it is successfully established, so that the investment can be realized and the money used for further projects.

Isla de Maipo

Subregion of Maipo, an enclave in a bend of the River Maipo. The home of VIÑA SANTA INES and VIÑA SANTA EMA and the site of the extensive La Caperana vineyard, reclaimed from the stony river bottom by Don José Cánepa.

Linderos, Viña

Viña Linderos was founded in 1865 by Don Alejandro Reyes Cotapos, a distinguished politician and president at different times both of the Senate and of the Supreme Court, and one of the first to introduce noble vines from Europe. Control of the firm later passed to the Ortiz family, and not so long ago Linderos was one of the better known Chilean wines abroad.

The different branches of the Ortiz family have since gone their own ways, and the wines are no longer exported.

Llano de Maipo

Subregion in the south of the region bordering Buin.

Manquehue Ltda, Viña DO w dr r
Av Vicuña Mackenna 2289, Santiago, Tel (2) 555 8565

Antonio Rabat Comella, the founder of Manquehue, was born near Vich in Catalonia. In 1902 at the age of 16 he sailed for South America, crossing the Andes into Chile on muleback, where, with an energy typical of the European immigrants of his generation, he started a successful bakery. He subsequently moved into the wine trade and in 1932 bought the farm of Santa Adela de Manquehue on the slopes of the hill of Manquehue (the name means 'The Place of the Condors') to the east of Santiago. Here he planted 150 hectares with vine stock brought from France and soon gained a reputation for his wines in Chile. 'Not even the grapes' breathing escapes me', he used to say.

When Don Antonio died, in 1955, he was succeeded by his son, the present owner, José Rabat Gorch. Faced with urban spread from Santiago, Don José sold the Manquehue vineyard and in 1980 bought land in the favoured areas of Pirque and Colchagua (in the Rapel Region). At the same time the firm thoroughly re-equipped its winery with stainless steel tanks, refrigeration machinery and American and French oak barriques. It is currently constructing a new plant in Colchagua.

The company has recently (1992) been reorganized, with Viña Manquehue supplying the domestic market (in which it is the fifth largest concern) with table and fine wines, bag in the box, wine coolers and an inexpensive carbonated sparkling wine. Wines for export, which have gained considerable success at international exhibitions, are handled by the associated concerns of DOMAINE RABAT and VIÑA SANTA ADELA.

Red Wine

'Santiago' Cabernet Sauvignon 1990 (tasted November 1992)
As supplied to Moreno Wines, London. 12° alcohol. Plum-ruby. Cabernet nose. Young taste, clean, full of fruit. Herbal, spicy and slightly resinous. Good finish. Would improve with another year in bottle.

'Medalla Real' DO w dr r res

Superior wines made by VIÑA SANTA RITA. The range comprises a Chardonnay, Sauvignon Blanc, Sauvignon Blanc Reserva, Cabernet Sauvignon, and Cabernet Sauvignon Reserva. The most resounding success of the Cabernet Sauvignon was at the 1986 Gault-Millau Olympiad in Paris, where the 1984 vintage beat all comers, including the Bordeaux First Growths.

Mitjans SA, Juan

Juan Mitjans 200, Santiago, Tel (2) 238 2511

Founded in 1903 by Don Juan Mitjans, newly arrived from Spain, the firm is still owned by the Mitjans family, which also controls VIÑA VALDIVIESO and Champagne Alberto Valdivieso. Mitjans makes a large range of sweet liqueurs (crème de cacao, crème de menthe, kirsch etc), as well as gin, vodka, anis and Chilean 'sherry' and 'port'. It also distributes the excellent 'Diaguitas' pisco.

Millahue Ltda, Vitivinícola see Portal del Alto, Viña

Mondragón, Vinícola DO w dr r

This is a subsidiary company of VIÑA CANEPA, marketing its very reasonably priced wines under the label 'Montenuevo'.

White Wine

'Montenuevo' Sémillon 1992 (tasted August 1993)
From the Maipo Valley. 13° alcohol. Pale lemon. Fresh, very light and clean, with taste of gooseberries and lichees and a hint of peaches. Long finish.

Red Wine

'Montenuevo' Cabernet Sauvignon 1991 (tasted August 1993)
From the Maipo Valley. 12.5° alcohol. Very dark plum. Lovely blackcurrant fruit and oak in the nose. Full-bodied and fresh with good blend of cassis fruit and oak and enough tannin to last. Long finish. First-rate young wine.

Ochagavía SA, Viña

Don Silvestre Ochagavía Errázuriz is known as the Father of the Chilean Wine Industry, since it was he who in 1851 founded Viña Ochagavía and embarked on the replacement of the traditional País in his vineyards with noble varieties brought from France, including the Cabernet Sauvignon, Merlot, Pinot Noir, Riesling, Sauvignon Blanc and others. Only 95 hectares of his original vineyards at Santa Rosa del Peral, 12 kilometres (8 miles) to the southwest of Santiago in the Maipo Valley, survive, and Viña Ochagavía was long ago taken over by VIÑA SANTA CAROLINA.

When, with Hugh Johnson, I visited the Chilean vineyards and wineries in November 1984, Santa Carolina marketed a range of wines under the Ochagavía label, including 'Gran Vino Exportación', 'Don Silvestre' and 'Antigua Reserva'. (Interested readers will find tasting notes in our book *Chilean Wines.*) Santa Carolina has latterly sold its best wines under its own name or that of the newly developed Casablanca, but I understand that there are plans to revive the honoured Ochagavía name.

Ortiz SA, Viñedos see Linderos, Viña

Pirque

Subregion to the southeast of Santiago in the foothills of the Andes, which has its origins in the purchase by Don Ramón Subercaseaux of the 5,920-hectare estate of the Hacienda de Pirque. The soil was then poor and arid, but by constructing a 5-league canal Don Ramón was able to irrigate it with water from the Maipo River and convert it into good agricultural land. He and his descendants, notably Don Melchor de Concha y Toro, planted the area with vines, and it is now one of the choicest areas in Chile for viticulture, with important holdings belonging to CONCHA Y TORO, MANQUEHUE and PORTAL DEL ALTO.

Portal del Alto, Viña DO w dr r res
Camino El Arpa s/n, Alto Jahuel, PO Box 1282, Buin, Tel (2) 821 3363

In 1968, Alejandro Hernández, Dean of the Faculty of Viticulture and Oenology at the Universidad Católica in Santiago and author of a number of authoritative books on Chilean wines, decided to put theory into practice and bought the property of San Juan de Pirque in the Alto Maipo area, adding that of Portal del Alto in 1970. The Cabernet Sauvignon from Portal del Alto is especially select, since the plants stem from French vines originally grown experimentally at the QUINTA NORMAL as early as 1850. Don Alejandro has more recently bought small vineyards in the Tinguiririca subregion of Rapel near San Fernando, where the winery is located, and near Cauquenes in the Maule Region, where the sparse soil and cool climate promise well for plantings of Chardonnay.

Portal del Alto's most successful wines are the Cabernet Sauvignon Gran Vino and Gran Reserva, which have received enthusiastic comment in the American *Wine Spectator* and *Wine & Spirit* magazines, and were highly commended in the *Wine* magazine 1992 International Challenge in the UK.

Quinta Normal

In 1838 the Chilean government purchased 25 hectares of land in Santiago for agricultural investigations. The first director of the Quinta was Claude Gay, who besides planting exotic trees and shrubs from abroad, carried out pioneer work in acclimatizing vines from France and Germany. The descendants of these stocks are much valued for their purity of strain. The wooded 40-hectare park is now a popular attraction, especially on public holidays, the Natural History and Railway museums as well as various recreational facilities being located there.

Rabat, Domaine DO w dr r

Vicuña Mackenna 2289, Santiago, Tel (2) 555 8565

When VIÑA MANQUEHUE separated its domestic and export operations in 1992, Domaine Rabat was one of the companies formed to make wines for export. It shares three vineyards with its sister ship SANTA ADELA: at Pirque (Maipo Valley), with 25 hectares of Cabernet Sauvignon, 17 of Chardonnay and 18 of Sauvignon Blanc; at Requinoa (Maipo Valley), planted in 1992–93 with 49 hectares of Cabernet Sauvignon, 16 of Merlot, 16 of Chardonnay and 40 of Sauvignon Blanc; and at Apalta (in the Colchagua subregion of Rapel), with 41 hectares of Cabernet Sauvignon and 12 of Sauvignon Blanc.

The wines have won considerable recognition abroad. The Cabernet Sauvignon 1989 gained a silver medal at Wine America 1992, and both the Cabernet Sauvignon 1991 and Sauvignon Blanc 1992 were named Best Buys by *Wine Spectator* in February 1993.

When tasted in May 1993, the 1991 Cabernet Sauvignon was somewhat closed, with subdued nose and flavour which opened out slowly in the glass.

Santa Ana

One of the most privileged subregions of Maipo, close to Santiago and just north of the Maipo. Its most famous vineyards are those of UNDURRAGA.

Santa Adela SA, Viña DO w dr r

Vicuña Mackenna 2289, Santiago, Tel (2) 555 8565

A sister company of DOMAINE RABAT, formed by VIÑA MANQUEHUE to make fine wines for export. It takes its name from the original Rabat property of Santa Adela de Manquehue, now engulfed by housing developments. The company shares some facilities with Domaine Rabat. Its Cabernet Sauvignon is made with grapes from vines planted 100 years ago by the former owners of the Apalta vineyard near Colchagua (Rapel), and is aged for four months in American barriques. The 1989 won a silver medal at Wine America 1992.

Santa Carolina SA, Viña DO w dr r res

Rodrigo de Araya 1431, Santiago, Tel (2) 238 2855

As mentioned earlier, Santa Carolina is one of the 'big four' Chilean wine companies and has been noted for the excellence of its wines since it was founded by Don Luis Pereira Cotapos in 1875. Don Luis, who was a wealthy mine-owner, a senator and minister of state, named the winery after his wife Doña Carolina Iñiguez. Like his contemporaries Silvestre Ochagavía and José Tomás Urmeneta, he was at the forefront of the development of the wine industry in the 19th century. He engaged two experts from France: the distinguished oenologist Germain Bachelet imported noble vine stocks and planted the vineyards, while the engineer Emile Duyère oversaw the construction of the underground cellars. Built of limestone and brick with mortar made of lime and egg-whites, these beautifully vaulted cellars are now a national monument.

Don Luis's original vineyard has long since disappeared amidst the ugly sprawl of the industrial suburb of San Miguel. The company now owns vineyards in the Maipo Valley at Santa Rosa del Peral and Plazuela de los Toros near Santiago, in the San Fernando Valley (Rapel), and in the developing Casablanca area near Valparaíso. It owns or manages more than 1,200 hectares, planted with Cabernet Sauvignon, Cabernet Franc, Malbec, Merlot, Pinot Noir, Chardonnay, Sauvignon Blanc, Sémillon and Riesling. The white wines are vinified in temperature-controlled stainless steel tanks or epoxy-lined concrete vats. The reds are fermented in stainless steel or large raulí vats and matured in small French or American oak barriques.

The wines are made by two talented professionals, María del Pilar González, and that rising star among international oenologists, the imaginative, charismatic (and at times temperamental) Ignacio Recabarren, who gained experience at Davis University in California, châteaux Margaux and Lafite, New Zealand's Cloudy Bay, and Australia's Coldstream Hills and Rosemount.

Santa Carolina is currently producing some of Chile's most exciting wines, and has won hundreds of awards for excellence since its first at the great Paris International Exhibition in 1884. Among recent awards are the Trophy of Honour and gold medal at VINEXPO 1989 for the 1982 Cabernet Sauvignon, the Gold Palm and gold medal at VINEXPO 1991 for the 1990 Sauvignon Blanc, and a cluster of awards for both white and red wines at the Sydney International Wine Competition in 1993. Its top labels are 'Santa Carolina' and 'Casablanca' (but see also Ochagavía).

White Wines

Sauvignon Blanc Reserva 1992

Made with fruit from 80-year-old vines in the Santa Rosa vineyard, Upper Maipo Valley. Cooled at night before fermentation. 90 percent fermented in stainless steel and 10 percent in small oak for four months, then blended. Pale lemon. Delicious restrained fruit in nose plus hint of oak. Refreshing and fruity – lichees, kiwi and gooseberries. Excellent balance; good acidity. Exceptional.

Chardonnay 1993 (tasted February 1994)

From the Maipo Valley, Los Toros vineyard. 12° alcohol. Little nose or flavour. Lacks concentration and fruit. Disappointing.

'Special Reserve' Chardonnay 1993 (tasted February 1994)

From the Maipo Valley, Santa Rosa vineyard. Fermented in stainless steel. 50 percent transferred to small French oak barriques; 50 percent given malolactic. 12° alcohol. Delicate Chardonnay and oak nose with hint of apple. Full-flavoured buttery Chardonnay taste. Good body and long finish.

Chardonnay 1992

First cooled in stainless steel, then fermented in two-year-old oak barriques, 50 percent French and 50 percent American oak. 20 percent left on lees for four months, the rest fermented for ten days and returned to stainless steel. No malolactic. 12.5° alcohol. Lemon yellow. Apricot nose with hint of oak. Luscious and fruity, following nose. Nice balance of fruit and wood. Good acidity and finish. Excellent.

Chardonnay Reserve 1992

From the Santa Rosa vineyard. 50 percent fermented in stainless steel and 50 percent in French oak (80 percent Vosges, 10 percent Alliers, 10 percent Nevers) for eight months. With malolactic fermentation. 12.9° alcohol. Lemon yellow. Intense and complex Chardonnay nose with overtones of pears, melons and wood. Full-bodied and round with buttery flavour. Almost meaty. A male wine which would go well with steak. Very, very good.

Red Wines

'Special Reserve' Merlot 1992 (tasted February 1994)

From the Maipo Valley, Santa Rosa vineyard. Fermented in stainless steel; aged for four months in two-year-old French barriques. 12° alcohol. Dark cherry. Fresh blackcurrant nose with touch of oak. Juicy and full-bodied – black cherries, cassis. Long finish with touch of tannin at end. Pleasant young wine.

Merlot Reserva 1990

From the Santa Rosa estate (Maipo Valley). Fermented at 27–28°C (81–82°F) in stainless steel. 20 percent aged in French oak barriques and blended. Dark cherry. Good concentrated Merlot nose and flavour with a hint of oak and some tannin. Very nice.

Cabernet Sauvignon 1989

Left on the skins for two weeks to augment tannin. 50 percent was aged in stainless steel for one year and 50 percent in French oak barriques. The wine was then mixed and kept in stainless steel until bottled in mid-1991. Dense plummy colour. Long legs. Lovely blend of fruit and oak on the nose. Sweet, mouth-filling berry fruit. Long finish. Excellent.

Cabernet Sauvignon 1988

From Plazuela de los Toros vineyard (Maipo Valley). 12.5° alcohol. Ruby with orange rim. Concentrated Cabernet Sauvignon nose – violets. Full blackberry and cassis flavours. Dry tannic finish. Long.

Cabernet Sauvignon Reserva 1991 cask sample

Fermented in stainless steel and left for three weeks on the skins, then matured 40 percent in stainless steel and 60 percent in French oak barriques (new, one-year-old and two-year-old Allier and Nevers). Bottled in October 1993 and to be given one year before release. Plummy colour. Long legs. Young fruity nose. Packed with sweet blackcurrant and blackberry fruit. Without, of course, the complexity of the previous wines, but should develop well.

Santa Ema, Viña DO w dr r

Izaga 1096, PO Box 17, Isla de Maipo, Tel (2) 819 2811

Pedro Pavone Voglino, the son of an Italian winemaker, left his native Piemonte for Chile in 1917. Like his compatriot José Cánepa, he bought land in the Isla de Maipo and began growing Cabernet Sauvignon, Merlot and Sauvignon Blanc, selling the wine in bulk to the large producers. In 1945 he and his sons, Félix, Bruno and Pedro Junior, decided to create and bottle their own brand, Santa Ema. By 1977 Félix, now in charge of the operation, bought another 320-hectare vineyard in the Cachapoal Valley (Rapel), some of which has been planted with Chardonnay in addition to the other noble grape varieties. The vines are densely planted to improve the quality of the fruit and are necessarily worked by hand and with horse-drawn ploughs. The winery, on the other hand, is equipped with stainless steel vats and modern machinery.

Santa Ema makes a Cabernet Sauvignon, Merlot, Sauvignon Blanc and Chardonnay. The wines are exported to Canada, the USA, Europe, and the other countries of South America. They have a good reputation and have won several international awards.

Santa Inés, Viña DO w dr r

Manuel Rodríguez 229, PO Box 47, Isla de Maipo, Tel (2) 819 2809

Pietro de Martino arrived in Chile in 1934 and, like his Italian compatriots, José Cánepa and Pedro Pavone of SANTA EMA, bought land in the Isla de Maipo. Here he found Sémillon, Cabernet Franc and a little Moscatel, from which he made wine which he sold to the big companies. Because of ill health, Don Pietro returned to Italy, entrusting the vineyard to his brother, Licinio. It was not until after the Second World War that Don Licinio was able to bring his wife, Armida Sforza, a descendant of the ducal family who were the patrons of Leonardo da Vinci, to Chile with their children. It was one of them, Giorgio de Martino Sforza, who extended the vineyards, modernized the winery and began making fine wines.

Santa Inés remains a close-knit family business, now exporting its Sauvignon Blanc, Chardonnay, Sémillon, Cabernet Sauvignon Blanc and Merlot to the USA, Canada, Europe, and the other South American countries. Its greatest success has perhaps been the 1991 Sauvignon Blanc, which won first place in the Wine America contest.

White Wine

Sauvignon Blanc 1992

Pale straw, bright. Fresh minty nose. Luscious fruit with flavours of mint and gooseberry. Good acidity and finish. Very nice, but without the body to stand up to food.

Santa Rita Ltda, Viña DO w dr (p) r res

Gertrudis Echenique 49, Santiago, Tel (2) 228 9166

There have been vineyards on what is now the Santa Rita estate near Buin, some 40 kilometres (25 miles) south of Santiago, since colonial days. At the time of the War of Independence they belonged to Doña Paula Jaraquemada, a staunch patriot, who hid General Bernardo O'Higgins, the future president of Chile, together with 120 of his men after their defeat by the Spaniards in

1814. The historic cellar where they took refuge has been renovated and turned into a museum; Santa Rita's '120' wines owe their name to the episode.

The founder of Santa Rita was Don Domingo Fernández Concha, senator and president of Chile's largest bank, who travelled to France in 1880 to acquire vine stock and equipment. He created the beautiful 35-hectare park and constructed the balconied house with its glassed-in *miradores*, connected with the chapel where the future Pope Pius X, a friend of the García Huidobro family, conducted mass during his stay in Chile with a papal legation.

By 1895 Santa Rita wines were being exported to Europe and the USA and they have since remained among the best from Chile. In 1978 the family sold the company; for a time it was 50 percent owned by the American glass manufacturer, Owens-Illinois. The other 50 percent was acquired by Don Ricardo Claro Valdés, a leading Chilean industrialist, who later bought out Owens-Illinois. He has since embarked on a large-scale expansion programme, both to enhance the quality of the wines and to increase production. The most spectacular developments have been the purchase of 8,000 French and American oak barriques for maturing the wines, the installation of stainless steel fermentation tanks and other modern equipment, and the purchase of 800 hectares next to the Buin winery, which is currently being planted.

The Buin estate will in due course be one of the single largest vineyards in Chile and, with existing properties, should be able to grow all the grapes for Santa Rita's wines. Present vineyards in the Maipo Valley, Lontué (Maule), Casablanca (Aconcagua) and Peralillo (Rapel) amount to 768 hectares, 420 of which are planted (or to be planted) with Cabernet Sauvignon, 156 with Chardonnay, 115 with Merlot, and smaller areas with Sauvignon Blanc, Pinot and Sémillon. The main winery is at Alto Jahuel near Buin, and there are smaller plants at Los Lirios (Rapel) and Lontué (Maule).

Santa Rita makes three lines of wine: 'Medalla Real' in Cabernet Sauvignon, Chardonnay and Sauvignon Blanc; 'Reserva' in Cabernet Sauvignon and Sauvignon Blanc; and moderately priced '120' in Cabernet Sauvignon, Merlot and Sauvignon Blanc. It has also introduced a premium and very expensive 'Casa Real' Cabernet Sauvignon of exceptional quality.

The wines have won various gold medals in the UK, the USA and elsewhere, and the reds are especially to be recommended. In October 1986 at the Gault-Millau Olympiad in Paris, the 1984 'Medalla Real' Cabernet Sauvignon won the highest marks of the 36 Cabernets entered, which included some French Premiers Crus.

Santa Rita is one of the main Chilean exporters, its largest markets being the USA, the UK, Canada, Denmark and Latin America. Sales of its quality wines are rapidly growing. For example, for the USA sales rose from US$842,219 in 1989 to US$3,330,855 in 1992.

White Wines

'120' Sauvignon Blanc 1993 (tasted January 1994)
13° alcohol. Slightly acidic with a little gooseberry fruit, but lacks concentration and spoilt by persistent sulphur.

'Reserva' Sauvignon Blanc 1992
From Maipo. Skin contact 14 hours. Fermented in stainless steel. No oak. 13.5° alcohol. Pale straw. Fresh, concentrated flowering currant nose. Light and fresh in mouth with taste of lichees, but a bit bland at the finish.

'Medalla Real' Sauvignon Blanc 1992
From Maipo. 10 percent aged two months in French oak. 13° alcohol. Pale straw. Oaky touch in nose. Floral but not as fruity as first wine. Lacks acidity.

'120' Chardonnay 1993 (tasted January 1994)
From Maule Valley. Partly barrel fermented. 13.5° alcohol. Pale straw. Some sulphur in nose and taste. Not a great deal of fruit. Straightforward buttery Chardonnay in middle and at end.

'Reserva' Chardonnay 1993 (tasted December 1993)
Pale lemon. Tropical fruit and oak. Luscious and full-bodied. Chardonnay comes through in the middle and at the end. Very nice.

'Medalla Real' Chardonnay 1993 (tasted December 1993)
From the Maipo Valley. Matured in French oak. 13.5° alcohol. Gooseberry and peach nose. Tastes of tropical fruit with touch of cedar wood, becoming more Chardonnay-like with airing. Good acidity at the end. Very pleasant.

'Reserva' Chardonnay 1992

From Maipo. Fermented 60 percent in American oak barriques and 40 percent in stainless steel. Four months over lees. 13.2° alcohol. Pale yellow. Straightforward Chardonnay nose and flavour with touch of oak. Fresh, but a bit neutral and lacking in acidity.

'Medalla Real' Chardonnay 1992

From Maipo. Fermented in French oak. Six months over lees. 13.4° alcohol. Pale yellow. Livelier, more intense. Good creamy fruit, long finish. Nice.

'120' Riesling 1993 (tasted December 1993)

Bright, pale lemon. Clean and fruity with quite good body and finish, but without much Riesling character.

Red Wines

'Reserva' Cabernet Sauvignon 1989

From Maipo. Nine months in American oak barriques. 12.3° alcohol. Deep cherry colour. Good fruit plus oak nose. Meaty with tannic finish.

'Medalla Real' Cabernet Sauvignon 1989

From Maipo. Ten months in French oak barriques. 12.5° alcohol. Black-currant nose with restrained oak. Round, mellow and attractive. Good balance and finish, with touch of pepper at end.

'Casa Real' Cabernet Sauvignon 1989

From Maipo. 18 months in French oak. Pretty ruby colour. Nice vanilla nose and fruit but the wine seemed very closed at the tasting. Over lunch, with time to air, it evolved noticeably in the glass, gaining in intensity. Another sample, drunk at dinner, was deep and well balanced, with intense cassis and blackberry flavours and long finish. A very superior wine.

Santiago

Subregion on the fringes of the country's capital which includes the famous wineries of CANEPA, COUSIÑO MACUL, SANTA CAROLINA and TARAPACA EX-ZAVALA.

Subercaseaux, Champagne   DO sp

The firm is named after Don Ramón Subercaseaux, whose daughter, Doña Emiliana, married the Marqués de Casa Concha, the founder of CONCHA Y TORO. It is owned by Concha y Toro and makes its sparkling wines at the firm's Pirque headquarters by the *cuve close* method (in Chile, any wine, as long as it bubbles, may be labelled 'champagne'). The base wine is made mainly from Sémillon and Riesling. It undergoes its second fermentation after the addition of sugar and cultured yeasts in pressurized stainless steel tanks, kept at 14–16°C (57–61°F) for four weeks, or at 10–11°C (50–52°) for six weeks.

The wines are good of their type, clean and fresh with fine-textured mousse. The 'Brut' has a little residual sweetness, and the 'Demi Sec' and 'Moscato' are definitely on the sweet side. The Moscatel is attractive, especially in the hot Chilean summer, with a very fragrant nose and varietal flavour.

Tarapacá Ex-Zavala SA, Viña   DO w dr r res
Av Los Conquistadores 1700, Piso 15, Torre Santa Maria, Santiago,
Tel (2) 232 4990

By the rather odd name, there hangs a tale. Founded in 1874 and planted with French vines by Don Francisco Rojas Salamanca, the vineyard was later acquired by the Zavala family. It seems (according to one account) that when Antonio Zavala divorced his wife she received the vineyard, but that he retained the brand name. Since this name was well known and all-important, she called in a shrewd lawyer, Don Arturo Alessandri, who resolved the problem by suggesting that she label the wine 'Ex-Zavala', tacking on the name of the province of Tarapacá in northern Chile from which he hailed. Don Arturo later became President of Chile and was known as 'The Lion of Tarapacá'. (I have read another equally circumstantial account, in which the vineyard-owner is named as Ricardo Salas Edwards. Untroubled by marital problems but careless about signing contracts, according to this story the unfortunate man agreed to pay 150,000 pesos, an astronomical fee at the time, before he realized how simple the solution was.)

When I first visited Tarapacá, in 1984, its 110 hectares of vineyards stretched back from the fine old stone-built cellars with their cedar wood rafters towards the slopes of the Andean foothills; and the red wines, which have always enjoyed a high reputation in Chile, were fermented in 8,000-litre oak vats. Since then, the vineyard has become an enclave in the residential areas of Santiago, and when the Compañía Chilena de Fósforos acquired the winery in 1992, it bought the 2,600-hectare estate of El Rosario de Naltagua in the Maipo Valley. During 1992–93 a first 330 hectares were planted with noble vine varieties, and the winery was thoroughly modernized with the installation of temperature-controlled stainless steel fermentation tanks, pneumatic presses and small oak casks.

Only one of the wines we tasted, the 1992 Merlot, was made by the new management, and it does not seem appropriate to comment on the 1987 and 1989 Cabernet Sauvignons, which had obviously been kept for prolonged periods in old wood and only very recently been bottled.

Red Wine

'Gran Tarapacá' Merlot 1992 (tasted July 1993)
Dark plum. Pleasant Merlot nose. Dry, tannic and very clean, tasting of chocolate with a hint of blackcurrant. Became softer and rounder with airing. Long finish. Nice.

Undurraga SA, Viña DO w dr r res
Lota 2305, Santiago, Tel (2) 234 1854

Undurraga is one of the best known Chilean labels abroad. This is largely because the firm was one of the first to export its wines, beginning with a shipment to the USA in 1903. Unlike most of the 19th-century pioneers, its founder, Don Francisco Undurraga Vicuña, did not make his fortune from silver mines or by exporting guano, but was an agriculturalist and landowner. Painter, poet and politician, he was nevertheless imbued with the idea of making Chilean wines to rank with the best in the world.

He began in 1882 by buying at public auction a property at Santa Ana, southwest of Santiago, near the junction of the Maipo and Mapocho rivers. This was in fierce competition with Doña Isidora Goyenechea of COUSIÑO MACUL, who arrived late at the sale and whose offer of an additional 100,000 pesos to buy it from him he firmly declined. Next, Don Francisco set about irrigating the land with water from a nearby canal and acquiring noble vines. He travelled to Europe in 1885, buying Riesling stocks in Koblenz, Frankfurt and Cologne, and Cabernet Sauvignon, Merlot, Pinot Noir and Sauvignon Blanc in France. The precious cuttings were packed in lead tubes and refrigerated so as to avoid budding during the passage through the tropics.

One of his most significant moves was over the selection and procurement of the wood for ageing his wines. While Overseer of the State Railways he ordered locomotives from Germany and flat cars from Bosnia and Herzegovina. His choice of this somewhat unlikely source was perhaps not unconnected, in his own words, with an awareness that: 'the wood from these parts is first class and very aromatic, and the Bosnian oak gives the wine a special fragrance . . .' At any rate, he was prompt to buy the wood in which the equipment had been shipped and to employ a cooper to make barrels from the staves. Some survive to this day and, according to Don Francisco's descendant and present head of the firm, Don Pedro Undurraga, are still used for maturing the famous and characterful 'Viejo Roble'.

Undurraga currently has 120 hectares of vineyards in the Maipo Valley planted with Cabernet Sauvignon, Cabernet Franc, Merlot, Pinot Noir, Riesling and Sauvignon Blanc, together with 180 hectares in the Colchagua subregion of Rapel with additional plantings of Chardonnay. The old bodegas are set in a park designed by the French architect Pierre Dubois, with well-watered lawns, decorative pools, long plumes of pampas grass, china blue plumbago, white and pink oleander, and purple bougainvillaea. Built in colonial style in 1890, with white adobe walls, orange-tiled roofs, wide arches and wrought ironwork, they have cool underground cellars which vary in temperature by only $2°C$ ($3.5°F$) the year round, with space for 4 million litres in American and Bosnian oak. The installations have lately been re-equipped and extended to house Vaslin and Bucher pneumatic presses, stainless steel fermentation tanks and temperature-controlled storage for 2 million bottles.

Undurraga is known for its traditional methods, but has recently acquired the services of one of the brightest and most forward-looking of Chilean oenologists, Fernando Ureta Cortes, formerly a professor of the Facultad de Agronomía at the Universidad Católica in Santiago. Over the years Undurraga has won scores of medals internationally, and under the meticulous management of Don Pedro Undurraga and his sons seems set to win many more.

A 'trademark' of the bodega is the flagon-shaped *caramayola*, in which its wines have traditionally been bottled, of the same shape as the *bocksbeutel*, and no doubt reflecting Don Francisco's admiration of German wines. They are still used for local sales and shipments to Germany and Denmark, but have been replaced by Bordeaux- and Burgundy-style bottles for all other markets.

White Wines

Sauvignon Blanc 1992

11.5° alcohol. Pale straw. Delicate floral nose. Flowery and round in the mouth. Lichees, flowering currant. Good acidity. Long.

Chardonnay 1992

Fermented in stainless steel and kept for 30 days in American oak. 11.5° alcohol. Pale straw. Subdued floral nose. Clean and refreshing with gooseberry flavour, but lacks substance and body.

Riesling 1992

Unfiltered. Fermented in stainless steel. 12° alcohol. Pale yellow. Clean varietal nose and flavour. Light. Sweet and sour finish.

'Viejo Roble'

Don Pedro had not included 'Viejo Roble' in the tasting and, when as an enthusiast I asked about it, he replied somewhat apologetically that it was not a wine in the modern style, but that Undurraga continued to make it because of massive demand in Chile.

It is made from Riesling and fermented in epoxy-lined concrete tanks, kept for two years in large barrels made from Don Francisco's original

Bosnian oak, and for one year in epoxy-lined concrete. It then undergoes cold treatment and filtration and is aged in bottle for not less than a year.

Bright lemon yellow. Oak plus fruit nose. Soft, clean, oaky and a good mouthful, although less full bodied than of yore. Good finish. Characterful and very nice.

Red Wines

Merlot 1992

Fermented in epoxy-lined concrete tanks. 11.5° alcohol. Full ruby. Fragrant Merlot nose. Damson flavour. Soft. Long finish with touch of pepper. Nice.

Pinot Noir 1990

Made with 85 percent Pinot Noir and 15 percent Cabernet Sauvignon. Matured in Bosnian oak. Deep ruby. Good berry nose with a touch of oak. Luscious and velvety with mellow blackberry and blackcurrant fruit. Long finish. There is not much Pinot Noir in Chile, and Undurraga makes the best. On our visits, we have always found the welcome flagon-shaped bottles entirely reliable and more than drinkable.

Cabernet Sauvignon 1990

100 percent Cabernet Sauvignon. Fermented in epoxy-coated concrete. No oak. Eight months in bottle. 11.5° alcohol. Dense ruby. Intensely fruity nose and flavour. Violets, blackcurrants and blackberries. Vigorous, meaty, long. Typical of a really good Chilean Cabernet.

Cabernet Sauvignon Reserva Selection 1988

Left in contact with the lees after fermentation. Matured for one year in epoxy-lined concrete then for two years in old Bosnian oak. 12° alcohol. Dense ruby. Very mellow strawberry with nice balance of fruit and oak. Herbal overtones. Finish long and a bit tannic. Very good.

Universidad Católica de Chile

There are two universities in Santiago, the Universidad de Chile and the Universidad Católica de Chile, and both have good oenology departments.

The Universidad Católica enjoys a particularly high reputation. The dean of its department is Professor Alejandro Hernández, who makes wine at PORTAL DEL ALTO and has written several authoritative books, including the recent *Wine and Vineyards of Chile*.

Although there is a growing influx of oenologists from France, the USA and Australia, most of those in the Chilean wineries have been trained in Santiago.

Valdivieso SA, Alberto sp w dr r
Juan Mitjans 200, Santiago, Tel (2) 238 2511

Valdivieso is a household word in Chile for its sparkling wines made by the champagne method (and unashamedly described by Chileans as 'champagne'), which account for 82 percent of the local market.

Its founder, Don Alberto Valdivieso, was a monied young aristocrat. He lived for long in Paris, acquiring a taste for French wines and champagne. When he returned to Chile in 1879 he modernized and expanded the small family winery with the help of French technicians. The Chardonnay he brought from France was the first to arrive in Chile and he planted it, along with Cabernet Sauvignon and Pinot Noir, in his Santa Elena vineyard near Santiago (most Chilean producers of his time canonized their wives and named their vineyards and wineries after them). His wines soon became known for their quality. Doña Elena and he were in the forefront of Santiago society and began supplying their Chardonnay to elegant friends on their 'private list'. So (as quoted by Fernando Ureta and Philippo Pszczólkowski in *Chile, Culture of Wine*), his diary for Independence Day, 12 September 1912, read: 'Elena and I bid farewell to the President who dined with us in honour of the festivities. With the first course, we served 'Chardonnay Reserva 1908'. His excellency celebrated our wine effusively and requested that we supply him with it at La Moneda Palace and his summer home.'

Don Alberto's lifelong ambition was to make a sparkling wine in Chile by the *méthode champenoise*, and in 1924 he achieved this by creating cellars specially for the purpose. The wine was a runaway success and soon *de rigueur* among the well-heeled of Santiago. In 1950 the Valdivieso family sold the company to the MITJANS group, another family concern. Mitjans has expanded the production both of sparkling and fine still wines by planting 120 hectares of vineyards at Sagrada Familia in the Lontué area (Maule) with Chardonnay and Pinot Noir, together with smaller amounts of Cabernet Sauvignon and Sauvignon Blanc. New vinification plants have been built at Lontué and in the Maipo and Aconcagua valleys, and are equipped with the latest in presses, cooling machinery, stainless steel tanks, oak barriques and so on from Germany, France, Italy and the USA. At the same time an Australian oenologist has been engaged to develop new-style white wines.

The *méthode champenoise* sparkling wines are made in the traditional way by dosing the base wine with cane sugar and cultured yeast, leaving the bottles in cool cellars until second fermentation is complete, slowly upending the bottles in *pupitres* so as to precipitate the sediment, expelling the sediment, and finally adding *liqueur d'expédition*, a solution of sugar in brandy and old white wine, before recorking. There are three types: Grand Brut, Nature and Brut, all made from Pinot Noir and Chardonnay. Sparkling wine is also made by the *cuve close* method in pressurized tanks in a brand new Charmat plant from Italy: the Demi Sec contains Pinot Noir, Chardonnay, Sauvignon Blanc and Riesling, the Rosé, Sauvignon Blanc and Cabernet Sauvignon, and a fruity and refreshing Moscato, 60 percent Torontel and 40 percent Moscatel.

Some 20 percent of the sparkling wine is exported. The still varietal wines are made exclusively for export, the traditional market being Latin America. However, ten years ago Valdivieso began exporting to the USA where it is now a major player, and exports to Europe began in 1993.

Sparkling Wines

'Nature' 1990

50:50 Pinot Noir and Chardonnay from Sagrada Familia-Lontué. *Méthode champenoise.* 11.5° alcohol. Pale straw. Clean biscuity nose. Lovely fruit. Fine mousse. Fresh and very dry. Long fruity finish. Excellent.

'Grand Brut' NV (tasted January 1994)

A clean, biscuity and slightly toasted sparkling wine which is refreshing to drink, but without complexity or depth of fruit. The mousse is somewhat short-lived.

'Brut' 1991

Made from 40 percent Chardonnay, 20 percent Pinot Noir, 40 percent Riesling, 8 grams residual sugar. Cloudy. Sweetish sulphur nose. Not much fruit or finish.

White Wine

'Chardonnay' 1992

From Lontué. Fermented 100 percent in stainless steel. 12° alcohol. Pale straw with green cast. Flowery nose. Sweetish at start. Clean, ripe Chardonnay. Light and a bit bland. Touch of mint at finish.

Red Wines

'Merlot' 1990

90 percent kept in stainless steel and 10 percent in French oak barriques for one year. Three months in bottle. Dark cherry red. Soft, luscious fruit with chocolate, liquorice and herbal flavours. Easy to drink.

'Merlot' 1989

From Maipo Valley. Kept for three months in large 10,000-litre French oak barriques. 12° alcohol. Dark cherry red. Chocolate nose. Fresh with good soft fruit and touch of cedar and spice. Long finish.

'Saint Morellon Cabernet Sauvignon' 1990

A blend of fruit from Maipo Valley and Lontué. 12° alcohol. Dark cherry. Blackberry fruit somewhat masked by oak. A less exciting wine than the 1989 below.

'Cabernet Sauvignon' 1990 barrel sample

From Lontué. Dark cherry. 15 percent aged in American oak barriques for six months. 12° alcohol. Dark cherry. Long legs. Vanilla scented. Fruity, well balanced, very soft and long.

'Cabernet Sauvignon' **1989**

From the Maipo Valley. Two years in large ten-year-old oak barrels of 10,000 litres, then seven months in 225-litre barriques. Ruby. Very nice Cabernet and oak nose. Round and very soft, with juicy blackcurrant/blackberry fruit. Good finish. Nice.

'Viejo Roble' DO w dr

An old-fashioned oaky white wine from UNDURRAGA, which despite its long sojourn in ancient Bosnian oak is surprisingly light, lively and character-ful. The Chilean public remains entirely faithful to it, and it would seem to be a valuable corrective to cleaner than clean, and lighter than light stainless steel varietals.

RAPEL

The Rapel Region lies between Maipo and Maule, bounded by the River Cachapoal to the north and watered by the Tinguiririca River in the south. There are ten subregions, from north to south: Rancagua, Rengo, Peumo, Colchagua, San Fernando, Santa Cruz, Cachapoal, Chimbarongo, Nancagua and Tinguiririca. The soils are mainly alluvial and the climate is subhumid with an average annual rainfall of 500–800 millimetres. Table grapes and wine grapes are grown in almost equal amounts. Of the wine grapes 4,545 hectares are red and 2,669 hectares white. The region's largest towns are Rancagua and San Fernando, and its well-known wineries include BISQUERTT, LOS VASCOS, PORTA, SANTA EMILIANA, SANTA MONICA and TORREON DE PAREDES.

'Andes Peaks'

A brand name of VIÑA SANTA EMILIANA.

Bisquertt, Viña DO w dr r

Andrés de Fuenzalida 66, Santiago, Tel (2) 233 6681

For five generations the Bisquertts have been growing grapes. About 15 years ago Osvaldo Bisquertt planted noble varieties chosen from the best in Chile in his Tinguiririca Valley vineyards between Palmilla and Peralillo. The area is particularly favourable, especially for red grapes, being frost free, very sunny in summer and wet in winter. Initially the fruit was sold to the large wineries, but four years ago Bisquertt began bottling and has since successfully exported to the USA and Europe. Some 140 hectares, of Cabernet Sauvignon, Merlot, Chardonnay, Sauvignon Blanc and Sémillon, are in production, and there are plans for a further 340 hectares. The red wines are fermented in large raulí vats, matured in French oak and kept in bottle for at least a year before being released. The Chardonnay is fermented in new 225-litre barriques of French oak, and new stainless steel tanks are being installed for the other white wines.

White Wine

Sauvignon Blanc 1992

From the Colchagua Valley. 12° alcohol. Pale yellow. Faint, but pleasantly fragrant nose. Clean and fresh with lemony flavour, but without much fruit. Good acidity. Elegant.

Cachapoal

Subregion in the north of Rapel lying along the Cachapoal River.

Chimbarongo

Subregion just south of San Fernando and the Tinguiririca River.

Colchagua

Subregion west of San Fernando in the Tinguiririca Valley. One of the 'coastal' valleys where LOS VASCOS is sited and firms such as SANTA RITA and UNDURRAGA have planted red grapes.

Los Vascos, Viña DO w dr r res

Isidora Goyenechea 3156, Santiago, Tel (2) 231 4372

The vineyards of Los Vascos were first planted in about 1750 by Don Miguel Echenique, a captain of dragoons in the service of King Fernando VI of Spain. His direct descendant, Doña María Ignacia Echenique, and her husband, Don Jorge Eyzaguirre Correa, continue the family's winemaking tradition. Two later forebears, Don Pedro Gregorio Echenique and Don Bonifacio Correa, were among the first Chilean landowners to bring back noble vines from France, with which the native País was replaced in about 1850. The property has remained in the family except for a period of expropriation during the Allende regime.

During 1975–79 the Eyzaguirres bought back the original holdings, together with plots from neighbouring smallholders. The estate now amounts to 2,200 hectares of which 220 hectares are under vines, 125 hectares consisting of 40-year-old stock and the remainder planted with 10-year-old vines. The family house, built low in colonial style around a patio full of roses, was devastated by an earthquake some years ago, but has been lovingly reconstructed and is one of the most beautiful country residences in Chile.

The vineyards are situated in the Cañetén Valley near Peralillo, about 40 kilometres (25 miles) inland. Sheltered by 900-metre (3,000-foot) mountains and free from frosts, on-shore winds result in a daily temperature change of 20–25°C (68–77°F), and the microclimate is ideal for viticulture. This and the high quality of the wines induced Château Lafite to buy a 50 percent share in Los Vascos in 1988. Since then, the winery has been extensively re-equipped with a 52-strong battery of 40,000-litre stainless steel fermentation tanks and large numbers of 225-litre barriques made in Lafite's coopery from Allier and Nevers oak. The wines are now made under the direct supervision of Lafite's Technical Director, Gilbert Rokvam, and are elegantly labelled with a Chilean version of the famous French original. Most of the firm's annual production of 2 million bottles is exported to the USA and Europe.

White Wines

Chardonnay 1992
No oak. No malolactic. Pale lemon. Clean Chardonnay nose. Luscious banana fruit. Pleasant finish.

Sauvignon Blanc 1992
Pale lemon. Flowery nose. Clean and refreshing with taste of flowering currant. Good acidity.

Red Wines

Cabernet Sauvignon 1991
7 percent press wine. Dark cherry. Blackcurrant nose. Intense blackcurrant/blackberry taste. Oak and ripe fruit balanced. Tannic – should last. Good finish.

'Grande Reserve' Cabernet Sauvignon 1991

50 percent matured in oak for six to eight months. Almost black with slight orange rim. Strong Cabernet Sauvignon nose with hint of oak. Rich, mellow fruit. Good balance and long finish. Very nice.

Cabernet Sauvignon 1989 (tasted November 1991)

Inky black colour. Deep fruity nose. Velvety chocolate and blackcurrant taste. Intense and long in finish. Beautiful.

This was the first vintage to be made by Château Lafite, beautiful at its best, but variable in quality, as were the white wines at the time. Of two cases of the 1989 Cabernet Sauvignon tasted, only a few bottles were of this standard.

Nancagua

Subregion in the Tinguiririca Valley west of San Fernando.

Peumo

Subregion west of Rancagua in the Cachapoal Valley. The largest holding is that of CONCHA Y TORO. In 1970 the company owned only 100 hectares of vineyards, but then bought another 3,000 hectares for development as vineyards and orchards (the juice from the freshly picked oranges is the best I have ever tasted). There are currently 383 hectares under vine, and the company employs about 600 workers on the estate and in a large winery with a capacity of 8.5 million litres.

Porta, Viña DO w dr r

Camino Antiguo S/N, Requinoa, PO Box 360, Rancagua, Tel (72) 237 142

Viña Porta is a small new winery, the creation of two Catalan brothers, Jorge and Carlos Gutierrez. The 65 hectares of vineyards at Requinoa in the Cachapoal Valley near Rancagua in the foothills of the Andes, planted with

Cabernet Sauvignon with some Cabernet Franc, Chardonnay and Sauvignon Blanc, supplied the grapes for the excellent 1987 and 1988 vintages of 'Montes Alpha' (see page 122). However, in 1990 the brothers joined forces with one of Chile's leading oenologists, Ignacio Recabarren, who reorganized the vineyards, supervised the construction of a state-of-the-art winery and shipped in oak barriques from the USA, Nevers and Tronçais. The following year, the Californian winery of Clos du Val and its oenologist Bernard Portet became involved. The first fruits were the excellent 1991 Cabernet Sauvignon and the outstanding 1992 Chardonnay, made partly with grapes from the granitic soils of Cauquenes in the foothills of the Cordillera de la Costa further south.

Unfortunately, Sr Recabarren withdrew from the venture after the 1993 harvest, and it is to be hoped that with the continuing involvement of Clos du Val the wines maintain their high standard.

White Wines

Chardonnay 1993 (tasted January 1994)
From the Valle del Maipo. 12.5° alcohol. Pale straw. The fragrant, honeyed nose tends to disappear. Full, round and intense Chardonnay in middle with overtones of lichees, papaya and peaches. Wonderfully complex in the mouth, soft and very long.

Chardonnay 1992 (tasted January and March 1993)
Made with 25 percent Chardonnay from Cauquenes and 75 percent from the Maipo Region, and aged in French oak. Honeyed nose – pineapple and tropical fruit. In its freshness the wine resembles a Sauvignon Blanc, but the flavour is of fresh Chardonnay with a lingering after-taste of tropical fruit. Lovely.

Red Wine

Cabernet Sauvignon 1991 (tasted June 1993)
12.5° alcohol. Dark cherry. Fresh, fruity nose with some oak. Intense blackberry taste. Round, tannic. Good balance and long minty finish. Very attractive young wine.

Rancagua

City and subregion. Rancagua lies 82 kilometres (51 miles) south of Santiago on the Pan American Highway and mainline railway. It is famous for the battle against the Royalists which General O'Higgins fought and lost in its streets in 1814. 'They covered us,' he wrote, 'with black and red, death and fire. So I took my banner, and I caused them to sew a black stripe across it; and the fire having reached the very house from which we were fighting, and our ammunition being all expended, we broke out through one of the squares which had been formed around our house, sword in hand.' It was after this that he and his followers took refuge in the cellars of SANTA RITA.

Rancagua is now a large city with a population of 143,000, the capital of the VI Region, and an important commercial centre at the heart of a flourishing fruit-growing and winemaking region. The most important winery in the adjacent subregion of the same name is VIÑA SANTA MONICA.

Rengo

Subregion south of Rancagua and to the east of the Pan American Highway in the foothills of the Andes. Its best-known winery is TORREON DE PAREDES.

San Fernando

Town and subregion. The town, 132 kilometres (82 miles) south of Santiago on the Pan American Highway and mainline railway, is capital of Colchagua Province, with 44,500 inhabitants. Some colonial relics remain in this thriving agricultural centre. West, the road to the coastal resort of Pichelemu plays leapfrog with a recently abandoned railway with crossings marked 'STOP', to be disregarded on pain of a fine to a lurking policeman, although there are now no trains! The road and railway link a string of wine towns, of which the main features are forlorn and massive stations and loading bays, including Placilla, Nancagua, Palmilla, Santa Cruz, Colchagua and Peralillo. SANTA EMILIANA has extensive vineyards and a large vinification plant in the subregion.

Santa Amalia DO r

The Santa Amalia vineyards in Requinoa, close to Rancagua, were bought some years ago by the Massenez family, makers of fruit liqueurs in Alsace. The oldest vines in the 160-hectare vineyard are being replaced with new stock; a start was made in 1991 with 20 hectares of Cabernet Sauvignon. They intend to produce fine red wines for export, and about 1,000 cases have already been shipped to the USA and Europe as 'Château Los Boldos de Santa Amalia'.

Santa Cruz

Subregion in the Tinguiririca Valley west of San Fernando, in which lie the vineyards of VIÑA BISQUERTT.

Santa Elisa Ltda, Sociedad Agrícola DO w dr r

Santa Elisa was founded in 1978 with extensive vineyards in the Rapel Region growing mainly Cabernet Sauvignon and Malbec with some Sémillon, Chardonnay and Pinot Noir, and a large vinification plant at Chimbarongo. It has since been taken over by CONCHA Y TORO.

White Wine

Chardonnay 1992 barrel sample
13.8° alcohol. Good body, flavour and acidity. Nice.

Santa Emiliana SA, Bodegas y Viñedos DO w dr r res
Fernando Lazcano 1220, Santiago, Tel (2) 555 5670

Santa Emiliana is named after the wife of Don Melchor de Concha y Toro, founder of the firm. For long part of CONCHA Y TORO, it became a separate company in 1986, although many of the original shareholders and directors remain. It owns nine separate properties totalling 1,800 hectares, located near Rancagua and San Fernando in the Rapel Region, together with 596 hectares in the Casablanca Valley. There are two modern vinification plants, one at Las Palmeras in the Tinguiririca Valley, the other in the Maipo Region, and four cellars with a combined storage capacity of 13.8 million litres.

Santa Emiliana markets a large range of wines, from bulk wines to blends and varietals and fine bottled wines for export. Its brand names are 'Santa Emiliana' and 'Andes Peaks'.

White Wines

Sauvignon Blanc 1992
From Rancagua and Rengo. 12° alcohol. Pale straw. Dry and clean with good acidity, but without much fruit.

Chardonnay 1992
Fermented in stainless steel. Five months in bottle. 12° alcohol. Little nose or fruit, but with reasonable acidity and pleasant enough to drink.

Red Wines

'Andes Peaks' Cabernet Sauvignon 1992
Made with 90 percent Cabernet Sauvignon and 10 percent Merlot from the Rapel Region at large. A fresh and very fruity young wine, still rather tannic. Easy drinking.

Cabernet Sauvignon 1992
100 percent Cabernet from Rancagua. Attractive Cabernet nose. Very mellow with masses of fruit. Good finish. Nice young wine.

Santa Mónica Ltda, Viña   DO w dr r res
La Lilas 625, Rancagua, Tel (72) 231 444

Viña Santa Mónica is very much a family concern. It is run by Emilio Solminihac and his wife, after whom it is named. The Solminihac family were fishermen from Brittany, and first came to Chile about 100 years ago to farm oysters. Sr Solminihac broke with tradition by studying as an agricultural engineer, returning to France to obtain an oenology degree at Bordeaux University. After setting up as a wine consultant in Rancagua, he bought the vineyards and winery of La Purísima outside Rancagua.

The 93-hectare vineyard is mainly Cabernet Sauvignon and Chardonnay, with smaller amounts of Sauvignon Blanc, Sémillon and Johannisburg Riesling. The old bodega has been modernized by cladding cement vats with epoxy, procuring French barriques from Allier and Nevers, and using sophisticated equipment such as vacuum filters – the first in Chile. The wine was sold in bulk to the large firms until 1981, when Santa Mónica began bottling and marketing under its own label. Exports of bottled wine began in 1989.

All the wine is made from fruit grown in the firm's own vineyards. It is of three types: Reserva de la Bodega; Envejido en Bodega; and the select Tierra del Sol, made with grapes from the oldest part of the vineyard with maximum exposure to sunshine and a yield of not more than 6,000 litres per hectare.

White Wines

Sémillon 1992

Pale straw. 13° alcohol. Pleasant flowery nose. Good fruit and finish.

Sauvignon Blanc 1992

Pale straw. 13° alcohol. Faint fragrance. Little fruit, but clean and refreshing.

Chardonnay 1992

Without oak. 13° alcohol. Pale lemon. Delicate Chardonnay nose and flavour, but without a great deal of fruit.

Chardonnay 1992

Fermented in French oak. 13° alcohol. Pleasant oak plus Chardonnay nose. Mainly oaky taste and finish.

Red Wines

Merlot 1992

Fermented in epoxy-coated cement. A third matured in raulí. Pleasant Merlot nose. Hints of chocolate and liquorice. Tannic and very dry. Had it perhaps picked up a touch of acid from the raulí?

Cabernet Sauvignon 1991

Fermented in epoxy-coated cement. No wood. 12° alcohol. Cherry red. Light, fruity nose and flavour. Pleasant, but lacks intensity and finish.

'Tierra del Sol' Cabernet Sauvignon 1988

Fermented in epoxy-coated cement. 12° alcohol. 18 months in French oak barriques. Dark cherry red. Good Cabernet nose. Rich fruit and good balance. Long finish. Nice.

Tinguiririca

Subregion lying in the valley of the River Tinguiririca, which runs from the Andes towards the Pacific along the southern fringe of the Rapel Region.

Torreón de Paredes, Viñedos DO w dr r res
Av Apoquindo 5500, Santiago, Tel (2) 211 5323

Amado Paredes Cardenas was 70 and the proprietor of a flourishing metallurgical company when in 1979 he bought a small vineyard at Rengo, south of Rancagua and at the foot of the Andes. The farmhouse, which dates from colonial times, has a splendid tower, hence the name 'Torreón'.

Don Amado and his two sons, who also gave up their professions – one as a lawyer and the other as an architect – have since toiled to extend and improve the vineyard. It has been progressively replanted with certified stock from the Instituto de Investigaciónes Agropecuarias, comprising Cabernet Sauvignon, Merlot, Sauvignon Blanc, Chardonnay and Gewürztraminer. In Don Amado's words: 'In this remote austral part of the world, the vine plants grow so beautifully and their fruits are so luxuriant and nice that they could well decorate the heavenly gardens.'

The Cabernet Sauvignon, aged for a year in French oak and for another in bottle, won a first prize at Wine America 1992 for the 1986 vintage. The same year a young Merlot won a gold medal at the Brussels World Wine Fair. The whole annual production of some 600,000 bottles is exported.

White Wines

Chardonnay 1992 (tasted June 1993)

From Cachapoal. 12.3° alcohol. Pale straw. Stylish Chardonnay nose. Very clean and fresh with beautiful fruit — kiwi, lichees and a hint of peaches. Finish a bit short and mild, lacks acid at the end, but very nice.

Sauvignon Blanc 1992 (tasted June 1993)

From Cachapoal. 12.2° alcohol. Pale straw. Flowery, but evanescent nose. Flowering currant in the middle, but the flavour disappears in the glass, leaving the wine flat and neutral.

Fumé Blanc 1988 (tasted June 1993)

From Cachapoal. Aged in French oak barriques. 12.7° alcohol. Faint attractive fragrance soon disappearing and giving way to oak. Clean, but little flavour or finish except oak.

In view of the exuberance of the Chardonnay, the last two wines were rather disappointing.

Red Wines

Merlot 1989 (tasted June 1993)

From Cachapoal. 12° alcohol. Plummy colour. Herbal, grassy taste — in fact, rue, with overtones of chocolate. Soft and round with ripe tannin. Long finish. Delicious.

Cabernet Sauvignon Reserva 1986 (tasted April 1993)

From Cachapoal. 12° alcohol. Dark cherry. Lovely fresh Cabernet fruit and nice touch of cedar. Beautifully fruity, soft and well balanced. The finish was good, but with a hint of dryness, and the wine eventually lost body and intensity in the glass.

This wine was so intriguing that we tasted another bottle. It differed entirely. It was well balanced with good fruit, a classy Cabernet Sauvignon, but closed and lacking the extraordinary fragrance and flavour of the first.

MAULE

This region occupies the middle of the Central Valley, extending from the rivers Teno and Mataquito in the north to the River Ñuble in the south. It is also watered by numbers of other rivers flowing from the Andes to the sea: the Lontué, Claro and Lircay, and the Maule, from which it takes its name. The soils are mainly alluvial in the north of the region; further south, they are derived from volcanic ash towards the Andes and are granitic on the western boundary in the foothills of the Cordillera de la Costa. The climate ranges from subhumid to humid from north to south with an average annual rainfall of 700–1,000 millimetres.

Table grapes are not as important as in Maipo and Rapel, and o f the grapes for wine, 14,925 hectares are red and 8,806 hectares white. The southern part of the region around Cauquenes is much favoured for growing white grapes, such as Chardonnay, because of the cooler climate and stony soils.

There are 11 subregions: Curicó, Lontué, Molina, Sagrada Familia, Talca, San Clemente, San Javier, Linares, Cauquenes, Parral and Villa Alegre. The main towns are: Curicó, Talca, Linares and Cauquenes.

Among the important wineries are: CALITERRA, CARTA VIEJA, DISCOVER WINE, SAN PEDRO and TORRES, together with a number of large cooperatives.

Agrícola Salve SA DO w dr r
PO Box 864, Talca, Tel (71) 242 506

Agrícola Salve (Societé Anonyme Les Vignobles) was founded in 1989 by the unlikely partnership of Michel Paoletti, a French wine connoisseur, Robert Wan, the world's largest producer of black pearls, his brother Louis, an entrepreneur from Papeete, and Julien Siu, wine-lover and gourmet, and owner of hotels in Tahiti. It is better known as Domaine Oriental, because the estate bought by the partners lies east of Talca.

The original vineyards had been planted with stock brought from France in the mid-19th century by the Donoso family. They now extend to 150 hectares, planted with Cabernet Sauvignon, Merlot, Sauvignon Blanc,

Sémillon and Chardonnay. The modern winery was planned by the gifted Alvaro Espinoza, now oenologist for VIÑA CARMEN, and is equipped with temperature-controlled stainless steel tanks and French oak barriques.

The winery currently makes a Sauvignon Blanc, two Sauvignon/Sémillons, one of which is partly passed through oak barriques, a Cabernet/Merlot, partly aged in American oak barriques, and an oak-aged Cabernet Sauvignon.

'Bellaterra'

Don Jaime Torres Vendrell was the first member of the Catalan Torres family to set foot on the shores of America, and it seems that when he first saw the coastline of the New World, he exclaimed: 'Quina Bella Terra!' ('What a beautiful land!'). This Sauvignon Blanc is named in his memory. Partly barrel fermented, it is aged in the same new oak barriques. This results in an intense and complex wine, with the oak giving it firm structure (see tasting note under Torres).

Caliterra, Viña DO w dr r res
PO Box 2345, Santiago, Tel (2) 228 1191

Viña Caliterra is a new winery founded in 1989 as a joint venture between VIÑA ERRAZURIZ and FRANCISCAN VINEYARDS of California. In 1991, the Chadwicks of Viña Errázuriz bought out Franciscan Vineyards, so that the enterprise is now 100 percent Chilean.

Caliterra owns 90 hectares of vineyard near Colchagua and in the Maipo Valley planted with Cabernet Sauvignon, together with 50 of Chardonnay and 37 of Sauvignon Blanc in the cooler Curicó area, where the vinification plant is also located. The balance of fruit is obtained under long-term contract with independent farmers, whose vineyards are carefully supervised.

The winery is one of the most modern in Chile. The white wines are fermented in stainless steel at temperatures as low as 12°C (54°F) and bottled early to conserve the fragrance and flavour of the fruit. A small amount of Chardonnay is part-fermented in American oak barriques, giving it more complexity. The very fruity Cabernet Sauvignon is fermented in stainless steel and then aged for 12–18 months in American oak barriques and for a further year in bottle before release. The largest market for the wines is the UK, and the quality/price ratio is among the best in Chile.

White Wines

Sauvignon Blanc 1993 (tasted January 1994)
From Curicó. 12° alcohol. Pale straw. Flowering currant nose. Herbal and gooseberry tastes. Fresh and clean, but unexciting. Lacks concentration.
Sauvignon Blanc 1992
From Curicó. Bottled two months after fermentation. 11.9° alcohol. Lemon yellow. Very fragrant floral nose. Tastes of lichees. Good acidity and finish.
Curicó Valley Chardonnay 1993 (tasted February 1994)
12.5° alcohol. Pale straw. Perfumed nose quickly disappears. Some Chardonnay flavour in middle. A fresh and clean wine, but lacking character and fruit.
Chardonnay 1992
From Curicó. Fermented in stainless steel. Pale lemon. Not very pronounced nose. Clean, pleasant and uncomplicated with reasonable fruit.
Chardonnay Reserva 1992
From Maipo. Fermented in American and French barriques. 12.8° alcohol. Deeper lemon yellow. More pronounced nose and more intense oaky Chardonnay flavour. Better acidity and finish.
Casablanca Valley Chardonnay 1993 barrel sample (tasted January 1994)
Intense Chardonnay and tropical fruit in nose. Concentrated flavours of Chardonnay, melon and papaya. Good acidity, long finish, beautiful.

Red Wines

Cabernet Sauvignon 1990
100 percent Cabernet Sauvignon from Maipo. 50 percent is oak-aged, 50 percent is not. 12.6° alcohol. Mid-ruby. Minty nose. Well balanced with touch of oak. Fruity and sweet. Pleasant finish.

Cabernet Sauvignon 1988
Kept for 18 months in American oak barriques. Dark ruby. Oakier nose.
Mellow with good blackcurrant fruit. Long finish. Very nice.

Carta Vieja SA, Viña DO w dr r res

Av Francisco Antonio Encina 231, Villa Alegre de Loncomilla, Tel (73) 381 612

The first del Pedregals settled in the Maule Valley in 1825 shortly after the
War of Independence and the family has been growing grapes and making
wine ever since. Don Alberto del Pedregal Aldunate is of the sixth generation,
and president of Carta Vieja; his two sons, Andrés and José Manuel, are in
charge of vineyards and production.

Situated in Villa Alegre de Loncomilla, south of Talca, the 350 hectares
of vineyards are planted with 133 of Cabernet Sauvignon, 150 of Sauvignon
Blanc and smaller areas of Merlot and Chardonnay; a further 120 hectares
will come into production in 1996. The winery, with a capacity of 6.5 million
litres in epoxy-coated concrete and 1.5 million litres in oak vats, is currently
being re-equipped and modernized. Outstanding are the barrel-fermented
'Reserva del Proprietario' Chardonnay and the 'Antigua Selección' Cabernet
Sauvignon, aged for six months in American oak casks and another year in
bottle. Of an annual 2.4 million bottles, half are exported. See also 'Valdezaro'.

White Wines

Sauvignon-Chardonnay 1993 (tasted September 1993)
12° alcohol. Pale lemon. Flowering currant nose, some sulphur. Chardonnay
in the middle and end, which are also lemony, but the sulphur persists.
Chardonnay 1992 (tasted May 1993)
12° alcohol. Pale lemon. Peachy Chardonnay nose. Full flavour of peaches
with a touch of honey. Good acidity and finish. Nice.
Chardonnay Reserve 1992 (tasted May 1993)
12° alcohol. Pale lemon. Peach and cinnamon nose. Peachy taste, buttery in
the middle. Acidic with good finish.

Red Wines

Cabernet-Merlot 1992 (tasted September 1993)

12° alcohol. Dark plum colour. More Merlot than Cabernet in the nose. Luscious, soft and plummy with chocolate and apricot flavours. Good finish. Nice young wine.

Merlot 1991

12° alcohol. Clean perfumed Merlot nose. Concentrated plummy taste. Brisk with somewhat short finish. Pleasant enough drinking.

Cabernet Sauvignon Reserva 1990 (tasted March 1994)

From the Maule Valley. 12° alcohol. Dark plum colour. Fruity nose. Good blackcurrant taste, but bone dry with the fruit masked by tannin. The wine is at the moment very closed, but should develop in bottle.

'Castillo de Molina'

Brand name for the premium Cabernet Sauvignon and Chardonnay from VIÑA SAN PEDRO. The Cabernet, which is aged for 12 months in French oak barriques and a further 12 months in bottle before release, was first made by Aurelio Montes and Douglas Murray, now of DISCOVER WINE, who for the first time in Chile imported French barriques for the purpose. The exportation of the first two vintages to Caymus of the Napa Valley (as 'Liberty School') and to France as 'Castillo de Molina' was a milestone in the recent history of Chilean wines.

Cauquenes

The subregion of Cauquenes is situated in the south of the Maule Region, west of Linares, in the foothills of the Cordillera de la Costa. The soils are granitic, and the hills are very much broken up and interspersed with alluvial valleys known as 'bogs'.

Because the rainfall is high (over 1,000 millimetres a year), the Cauquenes vineyards are generally unirrigated and planted mainly with the red País. In this zone, where the yield is often less than 3,000 litres per hectare, the variety produces pleasant everyday drinking wine; in irrigated areas with large yields, the wine is coarse. Because of its poor soils and lower than average temperatures, Cauquenes also produces small amounts of good quality Sauvignon Blanc, Riesling and Chardonnay, as well as a fragrant Moscatel.

The 45,000 hectares of vineyards are farmed by a host of smallholders, many of whom take their fruit to the large cooperatives of Cauquenes and Quillón for vinification. Recent studies and field trials by the Cauquenes substation of INIA (Instituto de Investigaciones Agropecuarias) and by FUNDACION CHILE at its ITATA vineyards have shown that with supplementary drip irrigation the Cauquenes area can produce noble grapes at least equal in quality to those grown further north.

Cauquenes, Cooperativa Agrícola Vitivinícola de DO w dr r
Av Estación Norte, Cauquenes, Tel (73) 511 026

This cooperative, one of the largest in Chile, was founded in 1939 after an earthquake had destroyed most of the existing wineries in the area. It is situated in the town of Cauquenes, west of Chillán in the foothills of the Cordillera de la Costa, only 25 kilometres (16 miles) from the Pacific. Its 260 members farm some 1.5 million hectares of unirrigated vineyards and 50,000 of irrigated land, mostly planted with the red País.

As in most of the cooperatives, the wine is fermented in concrete vats, coated with epoxy resin for making the better wines, and some of it is aged in large raulí vats and barrels. The bulk of production is inexpensive red País, which is sold in 5-litre carafes and litre bottles for local consumption. In fact, the País from the unirrigated area, unless spoilt by ageing in old wood, makes pleasant everyday drinking.

Under the label 'Lomas de Cauquenes' (*lomas* means 'slopes'), the cooperative also makes and exports much smaller amounts of bottled varietal wines. These include Cabernet Sauvignon, Riesling, Sauvignon Blanc and Chardonnay.

Curicó

Town and subregion. Located 192 kilometres (119 miles) south of Santiago on the Pan American Highway and mainline railway, Curicó is a bustling agricultural centre with 74,000 inhabitants at the heart of the wine country. It centres on the tree-lined Plaza de Armas, the former garrison parade ground. There are several hotels, but the pleasantest place to stay at is the Villa El Descanso, just north of Curicó – a restaurant, with chalets in the garden.

South of Curicó, is a band of soil derived from volcanic ash and continuing towards the Bío Bío Region. The well-known CALITERRA, DISCOVER WINE and TORRES wineries are located within the Curicó subregion.

Curicó, Cooperativa Agrícola Vitivinícola de DO w dr r
Balmaceda 565, PO Box 8D, Curicó, Tel (75) 310 047

Unlike most of the cooperatives, that of Curicó draws on grapes which are almost all grown in irrigated vineyards and are of noble varieties. Its members grow only 100 hectares of País as against some 620 hectares of Sauvignon Blanc, 430 hectares of Sémillon, 300 of Cabernet Sauvignon and smaller areas of Malbec, Riesling, Merlot, Pinot Noir and Chardonnay. The cooperative is well known for the quality of its wine and, bulk sales apart, the best varietal wines are bottled and sold under the name of 'Los Robles' or 'Gran Roble' as Cabernet Sauvignon, Merlot, Sauvignon Blanc, Sémillon and Chardonnay.

Discover Wine Ltda DO w dr r res
Apoquindo 3507, Los Condes, Santiago, Tel (2) 233 2854

Discover Wine (which makes the well-known 'Montes' wines) was one of the first of a new generation of small- or medium-sized wineries, sometimes called 'boutiques', devoted to making and exporting only high quality wine in limited amounts. It was established in 1988 by four partners, whose experience and skills range over the whole field of making and selling wine. Aurelio Montes, who has studied and travelled in Europe and California, was for many years head oenologist at UNDURRAGA and SAN PEDRO, and was the first Chilean winemaker to win a gold medal at VINEXPO in Bordeaux. Apart from making the wines, he contributes premium grapes from his own estate. Pedro Grand, a wine-grower of French extraction, is the owner of the Nogales estate which supplies most of the grapes for the wines, and also of the Nogales winery where they are made. The managing director, Douglas Murray, of Scots descent but born in Chile, began his colourful career with the Anaconda Copper Company before moving to Spain and looking after exports for leading wine companies in Jerez, the Rioja and Penedès. He returned to Chile as export manager for Viña San Pedro, where he was a colleague both of Aurelio Montes and of the president of Discover Wines, Alfredo Vidaurre, then chairman and executive director of San Pedro.

Most of the grapes come from the 85-hectare Nogales vineyards adjoining the winery. These are planted with 50 hectares of Cabernet Sauvignon, 20 hectares of Sauvignon Blanc and 15 hectares of Chardonnay, of which the average age is 20 years. Additional grapes from vines on average 50 years old are supplied from the estate of Aurelio Montes, also in Curicó. In the interests of quality, production is limited to 8,000–10,000 kilograms per hectare. Grapes for the Merlot are bought from neighbouring producers.

The old Nogales winery has been extensively modernized by the addition of a battery of temperature-controlled stainless steel fermentation tanks, together with modern pressing, cooling and filtration equipment.

Of the current annual production of some 900,000 litres, a large proportion is exported to Europe and the USA, and in the short life of the bodega the wines have already won numerous international awards. There are three labels: 'Montes'; the fruity and unoaked 'Villa Montes'; and 'Nogales'. The pride of the bodega is its 'Montes Alpha' which is made in limited quantity from the best and most select Cabernet Sauvignon grapes.

White Wines

'Villa Montes' Sauvignon Blanc 1993 (tasted July 1993)
12° alcohol. Pale straw. Very fragrant mint and apple nose. Light and clean

with tropical fruit in middle. With airing the nose and flavour become more peachy and melon-like.

'*Villa Montes*' *Sauvignon Blanc 1992*

12 hours' maceration. 12.4° alcohol. Pale straw. Fragrant gooseberry nose. Fresh and fruity with good finish and acidity.

'*Montes*' *Chardonnay Cuvée Ryman-Montes 1993* (tasted July 1993)

Made by the Hugh Ryman team. 12° alcohol. Pale lemon. Soft, fresh and very fruity – lichees, gooseberries, greengages. Good acidity and finish. Opens out markedly in the glass.

'*Montes*' *Chardonnay 1992*

Six hours' maceration. Barrel fermented. 12.3° alcohol. Lemon yellow. Good Chardonnay nose with gentle oak. Luscious taste of lichees, kiwi and pineapple. Long. Very nice.

'*Montes*' *Fumé Blanc 1992*

Made with Sauvignon Blanc. No maceration, three months in oak. 12.3° alcohol. Pale and elegant. Gooseberry taste with gentle oak and good finish.

Red Wines

'*Montes*' *Merlot 1991*

Without oak. 12.4° alcohol. One year spent in bottle. Deep cherry red, good Merlot nose. Marvellously fruity with chocolate flavours. Round, soft, juicy and concentrated. Long finish. A most attractive young wine.

'*Villa Montes*' *Cabernet Sauvignon 1990*

No oak. 12.1° alcohol. Very dark plum colour. Tastes of blackberries and mint. Round, soft and long.

'*Montes*' *Cabernet Sauvignon 1988*

Five months in oak. 12.4° alcohol. Fragrant Cabernet plus oak nose. Intense blackcurrant and blackberry fruit. Well balanced with long, soft minty finish. Excellent.

'*Montes Alpha*' *Cabernet Sauvignon 1989*

Very dark cherry. The bouquet bounces up from the glass. Intense blackberry fruit. Mellow and well balanced. Long finish with hint of tobacco. First rate.

'Montes Alpha' Cabernet Sauvignon 1988
One year in oak and six months in bottle. 12° alcohol. Dark ruby. Complex fruit and oak nose. Fresh and well balanced with lots of blackberry fruit. Long, long cigar box finish.

Domaine Oriental see Agrícola Salve SA

Echeverría, Viña DO w dr r
Av A Vespucio Norte 568, Dept 701, Santiago, Tel (2) 206 2786

The Echeverría family has been growing and making wines for some 250 years. The estate and winery are situated on the outskirts of the town of Molina, just south of Curicó and to the east of the Pan American Highway. The 70 hectares of vineyards are planted with Cabernet Sauvignon (50 percent), Sauvignon Blanc (30 percent) and Chardonnay (20 percent).

Until recently Don Roberto Echeverría, who himself makes the wine, has sold it in bulk to the large firms. However, since 1993 he has begun to bottle the wines and sell them under his own label as Chardonnay, Sauvignon Blanc and Cabernet Sauvignon. The following tasting note is on a bulk sample of the 1993 Sauvignon Blanc.

White Wine
Sauvignon Blanc 1993
12° alcohol. Very nice, fragrant, almost Riesling-like nose. Kiwi fruit and flowering currant flavours in middle. Clean, light and refreshing, but both the nose and taste tended to disappear in the glass.

Exposición, Vinos see Talca, Cooperativa Agrícola Vitivinícola de

'Gato Blanco', 'Gato Negro'

Brand names for big-selling Sauvignon Blanc and Cabernet Sauvignon wines from VIÑA SAN PEDRO, with their colourful labels depicting a crouching cat.

INIA Subestación Experimental Cauquenes

The Cauquenes experimental station of the government-run Instituto de Investigaciones Agropecuarias is one of a number covering the whole of the country. It is particularly concerned with fruit-growing and viticulture in the VII Region and possesses vineyards and an experimental winery. Its investigations have centred on the drip irrigation of vines and the possibilities for growing noble varieties in the Cauquenes area. The conclusion is that with supplementary irrigation and adequate technical and financial infrastructures the region is capable of producing wines as good as any in Chile.

Linares

Town and subregion in the south of the Maule Region west of Cauquenes. The town of Linares is 310 kilometres (193 miles) south of Santiago on the Pan American Highway and mainline railway.

'Lomas de Cauquenes'

Brand name of the better bottled wines made by the COOPERATIVA AGRICOLA VITIVINICOLA DE CAUQUENES.

Loncomilla, Cooperativa Agrícola Vitivinícola de w dr r

The cooperative is located in the Loncomilla Valley west of Linares. 75 percent of the grapes are from unirrigated vineyards in the foothills of the Cordillera de la Costa and almost all are País. The white wines are made from

1 2 3

a blend of Cabernet Sauvignon and Sémillon grown in the Irrigated Zone. Of the cooperative's production, 90 percent is sold in bulk.

Lontué

Subregion in the valley of the Lontué River, just south of Curicó. A number of well-known firms, including SAN PEDRO, SANTA RITA and VALDIVIESO, own vineyards in this most privileged area.

'Los Robles'

Brand name for the better bottled wines made by the COOPERATIVA AGRICOLA VITIVINICOLA DE CURICO.

'Manso de Velasco'

Premium Cabernet Sauvignon from MIGUEL TORRES, made with dark, compact bunches of grapes from a small number of 100-year-old vines, which yield a particularly complex wine. It is named in honour of José Antonio Manso de Velasco, who founded the city of Curicó in 1743 and was its first governor.

Molina

Subregion lying between the rivers Teno and Claro, south of Curicó and adjoining the subregion of Lontué. The large firm of VIÑA SAN PEDRO has its main winery and extensive vineyards here.

'Montes'

Brand name for a range of excellent wines from DISCOVER WINE, named after its oenologist Aurelio Montes.

Parral

Subregion in the valley of the Ancoa River southwest of Linares.

Sagrada Familia

Subregion in the Mataquito Valley west of Curicó, in which VIÑA ERRAZURIZ and VIÑA CANEPA have extensive vineyards.

San Clemente

Subregion southeast of Talca in the foothills of the Andes with soils derived from volcanic ash. Its best-known winery is CARTA VIEJA.

San Javier

Subregion in the foothills of the Cordillera de la Costa southwest of Talca at the confluence of the Maule and Claro rivers.

San Pedro SA, Viña w dr r res g
Aysen 115, Santiago, Tel (2) 238 1537

In its origins Viña San Pedro dates back to 1701, when Don Cayetano Correa acquired flat, well-irrigated land near the village of Molina, which he planted with País. The present concern resulted from the merger in 1845 of adjoining farms belonging to the Correa Albano brothers and their subsequent journey to France to acquire Cabernet Sauvignon and Sauvignon Blanc. Chardonnay and Merlot were also planted after a later visit.

At the turn of the century the Correa Albano family engaged the eminent French oenologist, Professor M Pacottet, who in 1907 designed and installed at San Pedro the world's first refrigeration unit for treating wines. A further example of enterprise was the bulk shipment in 1958 in the tanker *Charlton Venus* of 10.7 million litres of wine to France — Chile's largest ever single export. Meanwhile the Correa family had in 1941 sold the company to the family-owned concern of Wagner, Stein, which in 1982 disposed of it to a Chilean investment company working in partnership with the octopus-like Spanish conglomerate, RUMASA. Experiments such as the blending of Chilean wine with cheap Spanish Mancha marked a low in the fortunes of San Pedro, which ended with the expropriation of RUMASA by the Spanish government and the takeover of the winery by the Chilean State Bank. It has since been returned to private ownership and has resumed a successful role as one of the 'big four' Chilean wine companies. As of the end of 1993, San Pedro had 913 hectares of vineyards in the Lontué Valley under vines, planted with:

Cabernet Sauvignon	352 ha
Sauvignon Blanc	329 ha
Chardonnay	116 ha
Merlot	97 ha
Sémillon	10 ha
Riesling	7 ha
Cabernet Franc	2 ha

There are two large wineries. The vinification plant at Molina, on the land bought by Don Cayetano Correa so many years ago, is being re-equipped with stainless steel and small oak casks. A second plant, at Lontué, is basically devoted to storage and bottling.

San Pedro has a 27 percent share of the domestic market with annual sales equivalent to 2,650,000 cases. An interesting development is the use of 'tetra-packs' instead of returnable bottles, which now account for 70 percent of home sales. Exports of fine wines to five continents have risen from 27,050 cases in 1983 to 1 million in 1993.

The Bordeaux-based Jacques Lurton has recently been appointed consultant to the winery. As from the 1994 harvest he is supervising all winemaking at Viña San Pedro, while Brett Jackson, a New Zealand winemaker belonging to the Lurton team, is to be permanently based at the winery. Future wines are therefore likely to be significantly different in style.

White Wines

'Siglo de Oro' Chardonnay 1993 (tasted January 1994)
From the Curicó Valley. Subdued Chardonnay nose. Clean, very light, little body or fruit and lacks intensity.

Chardonnay 1992
Macerated for 12–15 hours before fermentation. Aged in new French oak barriques for three months. No malolactic. 13° alcohol. Pale straw. Not very pronounced Chardonnay masked by a touch of sulphur. Hint of gooseberries. Good acidity.

'Castillo de Molina' Chardonnay 1993 (tasted January 1994)
12.3° alcohol. Barrel fermented. Faint honeyed nose. Delicate, mainly oaky taste. Astringent at finish and lacks concentration.

'Castillo de Molina' Chardonnay 1992
From Lontué. Macerated for 12 hours before fermentation in new French oak barriques. 100 percent malolactic. 12° alcohol. Pale straw. Chardonnay more marked in the middle than in the nose. Gentle oak. A bit short on fruit and finish.

'Gato Blanco' Sauvignon Blanc 1992
12° alcohol. Very pale straw. Slight mercaptan in the nose. Little fruit and rather neutral.

'Santa Helena Siglo de Oro' Sauvignon Blanc 1992
100 percent Sauvignon Blanc. Macerated for 12–15 hours before fermentation. 12° alcohol. Pale straw. Floral nose with touch of sulphur. Not much fruit or varietal character – faint gooseberry. Smoky finish, but short.

'Santa Helena Selección del Directorio' Sauvignon Blanc 1993 (tasted January 1994)
From the Curicó Valley. Little nose. Subdued gooseberry taste. Touch of sweetness in middle. Light to a degree.

'Santa Helena Selección del Directorio' Sauvignon Blanc 1992

100 percent Sauvignon Blanc. 50 percent fermented in stainless steel and 50 percent in new American oak barriques. Four months' maturation in cask. 12° alcohol. Delicate fruit plus oak nose. Tastes mostly of oak with a little fruit. Short finish. The best of the white wines, but all are on the light side. Note, however, that 40–45 percent of the 1992 harvest was lost through frost, and the white grapes in particular were heavily damaged.

Red Wines

'Gato Negro' Cabernet Sauvignon 1991

100 percent Cabernet Sauvignon. Grape must added after fermentation. 12.5° alcohol. 5 grams per litre of residual sugar. Quite good blackcurrant taste. Smooth. Pleasant young commercial wine.

'Santa Helena Gran Vino' Cabernet Sauvignon 1990

100 percent Cabernet Sauvignon from pergolas. No wood. Left on skins for ten days. 11.5° alcohol. Deep ruby. Blackcurrants and cherries. Juicy, uncomplicated and easy drinking. Nice.

Santa Helena Siglo de Oro Cabernet Sauvignon 1989

12° alcohol. 33 percent aged in a mixture of French and American oak barriques for six months. Dark cherry. Pleasant blend of fruit and oak, but fruit not as intense as in the 'Gran Vino'.

Cabernet/Merlot 1992

The wines are blended after fermentation. 30 percent aged in American oak for three months. 12.4° alcohol. Inky plum colour. Pronounced oak and mainly Merlot nose. Tannic. Intense fruit and chocolate taste. Nice.

Cabernet/Merlot 1990

Wines blended as above. 12.6° alcohol. Deep ruby. Fruity with good finish. Pleasant, but not as intense as the 1992.

Merlot 1991

100 percent Merlot. 25 percent aged in American oak for six months. Dark cherry. Merlot taste with chocolate and tobacco flavours, but a little closed and very oaky at the finish. (This wine has been enormously successful abroad.)

'Castillo de Molina' Cabernet Sauvignon 1988

100 percent Cabernet Sauvignon, aged for one year in French oak barriques and for a further year in bottle. Dense ruby colour. Pronounced legs. A big wine – soft, round and minty, well balanced and with a long finish. Very nice.

'Santa Helena Selección del Director' Cabernet Sauvignon 1988

100 percent Cabernet Sauvignon, aged for nine months in American oak barriques. Almost black. Cigar box nose. Intense fruit – violets, chocolate. Full-bodied, well balanced, complex; wonderful long finish. The best of the reds.

'Santa Digna'

Brand name for superior Sauvignon Blanc, Rosé and Cabernet Sauvignon wines from MIGUEL TORRES.

'Santa Helena'

Brand name for a range of good quality wines from VIÑA SAN PEDRO, of which the 'Selección del Director' are the best. The Cabernet Sauvignon is outstanding.

Segu Ollé y Cía Ltda

Yumbel 383, PO Box 72, Linares, Tel (73) 210 078

Segu Ollé is a family firm established in 1924 by three Catalan winemakers, whose descendants continue the business. The winery and 185 hectares of vineyards lie in the Melozal Valley, 30 kilometres (19 miles) west of Linares between the Loncomilla River and the Cordillera de la Costa and are planted with Cabernet Sauvignon, Chardonnay, Sauvignon Blanc, Gewürztraminer, Riesling, Moscatel, Carignan and País. The annual yield is 1.5 million litres and the wines are bottled under the name 'Caliboro'.

Talca

City and subregion. Talca is the capital of the VII Region and, with a population of 140,000, is the most important town between Santiago and Concepción. It lies 258 kilometres (160 miles) south of Santiago on the Pan American Highway and mainline railway. It was founded by the Spaniards in 1662, and it was here that Chilean independence was declared in 1818. Flattened by earthquakes in 1742 and 1928, Talca has been completely rebuilt and is today a handsome, modern city. Not least of its attractions is the large open market, with its flower-sellers and stalls selling wickerwork, pottery and the best selection of straw hats I have ever encountered.

Apart from large-scale production of wine and cereals, the province of Talca is the home of the *guasos*, the traditional Chilean cowhands. The subregion lies at the centre of the Maule Region in the valley of the River Lircay.

Talca, Cooperativa Agrícola Vitivinícola de DO w dr r sp
Avda San Miguel 2631, PO Box 394, Talca, Tel (73) 242 342

This large cooperative was founded in 1944 and, unlike those situated further west, the larger part of the land farmed by its members (some 65 percent) is irrigated and planted with noble varieties. It numbers 75 *socios* or members, who between them cultivate 1,300 hectares of vineyard, planted with 25 percent Cabernet Sauvignon, 20 percent Sauvignon Blanc, 20 percent Sémillon and 35 percent País. The cooperative also vinifies the grapes from another 50 smallholders owning a further 850 hectares of vineyards.

Of the production, 60 percent is sold in bulk to large firms, including CONCHA Y TORO, SANTA RITA and SANTA CAROLINA; 30 percent is bottled for the domestic market; and 10 percent is exported, either in bulk or bottle, to the USA, Canada and Europe.

The best wines are labelled 'Vinos Exposición' (Sauvignon Blanc, Sémillon Blanc, Sémillon/Sauvignon, Rosé, Cabernet Sauvignon, Cabernet/ Merlot). There is also a 'Conde del Maule' sparkling wine, made by the *cuve close* method.

Torres SA, Vinícola Miguel DO w dr r res sp
Panamerican Sur Km 195, Curicó, Tel (75) 310 455

It seems fitting that when Miguel Torres, the largest exporter of Spanish beverage wines, decided to make wines outside Spain, the first choice was South America. More than a century earlier, a younger son of the Torres family had emigrated and prospered in Havana. The firm of Torres was founded when the émigré joined forces with his elder brother, Miguel; and in its earlier days a large part of the company's business was with South America. Having investigated a number of areas, their descendant Miguel A Torres decided on the Curicó area of Chile, preferring it to the more northerly part of the Central Valley because the average temperatures are 2°C lower than in the Santiago region and more suited to growing white grapes. In 1978 Torres bought the small Maquehua bodega of the Ahrex family, together with its 100 hectares of vineyard. By 1979 the replanting of the vineyards with Cabernet Sauvignon, Chardonnay, Riesling, Gewürztraminer and other noble varieties was well under way, as was the re-equipping of the bodega with stainless steel fermentation tanks, brought from Catalonia, pneumatic presses, cooling equipment and small American and French oak casks for ageing the wines.

In hindsight, the arrival of Miguel Torres, one of the world's leading and most innovative winemakers, marked the beginning of a new era for Chilean wines. Until then, both reds and whites had been aged for long periods in old raulí barrels. Torres began making young, fruity varietals by fermenting the grapes at controlled temperatures in stainless steel. Other departures were: the strict limitation of yield to no more than 10,000 litres per hectare; the *coupage* of wines fermented partly in stainless steel and partly in small oak casks; the strictest hygiene in the winery; and the storage of white wines at a low temperature and bottling shortly prior to despatch. By example and in sharing his expertise with other wineries, Miguel Torres has made a major personal contribution. It is characteristic of the man that all the profits from the Chilean operation have been ploughed back into improvements in the vineyards and bodega (in prudent Catalan fashion, the stainless steel tanks are not bought ready-made; the components are shipped from Catalonia and assembled *in situ*).

Torres now owns 230 hectares of vineyards near Curicó and in the Lontué Valley. A wide range of varieties is grown: Sauvignon Blanc, Riesling, Gewürztraminer and Chardonnay for the whites; Cabernet Sauvignon and Merlot for the red and rosé wines; as well as a little Pinot Noir and Malbec. The vines are planted in carefully chosen locations; at the Maquehua farm, for example, the white grapes are grown in the stony bed of the Guaiquillo River. At harvest time and before fermentation, there is careful sampling and tasting of the grapes from different stock and areas of the vineyards to ensure the best results.

The white wines comprise: the 'Don Miguel' Riesling/Gewürztraminer; 'Santa Digna' Sauvignon Blanc; 'Bellaterra' Sauvignon Blanc, partly barrel fermented then aged in the same new oak barriques; and 'Chardonnay de la Cordillera', partly barrel fermented and aged for four to five months in new oak barriques. The youthful 'Santa Digna' rosé is made with Cabernet Sauvignon and given short skin contact for structure and colour. The outstanding 'Manso de Velasco' Cabernet Sauvignon is made with fruit from an old single vineyard, and there is also a younger 'Santa Digna'. A further departure is the most attractive 'Brut Nature' sparkling wine made from a classical blend of 75 percent Chardonnay and 25 percent Pinot Noir by the traditional champagne method.

Current annual production is some 1.4 million bottles, of which 70 percent is exported. There are no plans for increasing this, the aim of the bodega being to produce only fine wines in limited quantity. The wines have won gold and silver medals at Olympia and at other international exhibitions.

White Wines

'Santa Digna' Sauvignon Blanc 1993 (tasted February 1994)
13.5° alcohol. Fermented in stainless steel. Very pale straw. Beautifully flowery nose with overtones of fennel, apple and tropical fruit. Tastes of peaches and tropical fruit. Long finish with touches of astringency.

Sauvignon Blanc 1992

12° alcohol. Very pale straw. Delicate floral nose. Gooseberry taste. Light and very clean with good finish.

'Bellaterra' Sauvignon Blanc 1992

Fermented in new American oak barriques. 14° alcohol. Pale straw. Floral nose with overtones of oak. Complex and fruity – quince and lemon verbena – with long finish.

'Chardonnay de la Cordillera' 1993 (tasted January 1994)

70 percent fermented in stainless steel and 30 percent in Nevers oak, then matured over the lees in cask until bottled. 13.5° alcohol. Beautiful flowery Chardonnay nose with gentle oak. Full Chardonnay flavour with overtones of lichees. Harmonious, excellent balance with good acidity and finish. Very nice.

Chardonnay de la Cordillera 1992

25 percent barrel fermented in Nevers oak barriques. 13.5° alcohol. Pale lemon with greenish cast. Flowery nose. Strong Chardonnay flavour in middle. Good acid. Clean and light with long finish. Very, very good.

'Don Miguel' Riesling and Gewürztraminer 1993 (tasted February 1994)

From Curicó district. 12.5° alcohol. Pale straw. Ethereal nose with touch of herbs. Bitter-sweet flavour – honey and flowers, hyacinth, water lily. Good finish, slightly peppery at end. Elegant.

'Don Miguel' Riesling/Gewürztraminer 1992

Half-and-half Riesling and Gewürztraminer. Pale straw. Concentrated floral bouquet. Light, crisp and fruity, especially at the end.

Rosé Wines

'Santa Digna' Cabernet Sauvignon Rosé 1993 (tasted January 1994)

From Curicó. 12.5° alcohol. Onion skin. Delicate floral nose. Light clean and astringent, but without a great deal of fruit. Hint of strawberry at finish.

'Santa Digna' Cabernet Sauvignon Rosé 1992

Left on the skins overnight. No oak. Pale onion skin. Delicately fruity. Light, crisp and slightly vegetal.

Red Wines

'Santa Digna' Cabernet Sauvignon 1990

100 percent Cabernet Sauvignon. 12 months in oak. Ruby. Very fragrant Cabernet nose. Blackcurrant and cinnamon flavours. Soft and well balanced with good tannins at finish.

'Manso de Velasco' Cabernet Sauvignon 1987

Made with specially selected grapes from an old single vineyard. Aged in Nevers oak. Very dark cherry. Mature Cabernet nose. Rich, intense and beautifully balanced, with ripe tannins and long finish.

Urmeneta

A wealthy owner of silver mines, José Tomás Urmeneta was one of the first to plant French vines in Chile, and the Urmeneta wines were among the best known in Chile during the latter part of the 19th century. The name survives as one of the labels of VIÑA SAN PEDRO.

'Valdezaro'

Label used by VIÑA CARTA VIEJA for a range of inexpensive blended wines.

Villa Alegre

Subregion north of Linares between the Maule and Loncomilla rivers and the home of VIÑA CARTA VIEJA.

BIO BIO

The southernmost of the demarcated regions, Bío Bío, lies between the Ñuble River in the north and the Bío Bío in the south. The average annual rainfall of 1,200–1,500 millimetres is considerably higher than that of the other regions, and the median temperature of 13–14°C (55–57°F) is lower. There is little production of table grapes, and of those for making wine some 17,000 hectares are planted with red grapes, 10,000 hectares with white. The predominant vine variety is the native País, grown in the unirrigated area which borders the Cordillera de la Costa.

There are five subregions: Ñuble, Chillán, Coelemu, Quillón and Yumbel. The principal towns are Concepción, Chillán and Los Angeles. Beyond the southern limits of this region, the climate is too harsh to grow vines.

Chillán

City and subregion, situated 407 kilometres (253 miles) south of Santiago on the Pan American Highway and mainline railway, Chillán is an important agricultural centre, with 133,000 inhabitants. It was the birthplace of Chile's national hero Bernardo O'Higgins, but virtually nothing of its past survives, since it was destroyed by earthquakes in 1833, 1939 and 1960. Nevertheless, it is a pleasant modern city with an attractive central square and a cathedral noted for its murals. In the Andes to the east, there is good skiing on the slopes of the Volcano of Chillán. The subregion lies in the valley of the Ñuble River.

Coelemu

Subregion east of Chillán lying in the Itata Valley, where the river traverses the Cordillera de la Costa on its way to the Pacific.

Concepción

Concepción, capital of the VIII Region, 519 kilometres (323 miles) from Santiago and 15 kilometres (9 miles) from the mouth of the Bío Bío River, is the most important city in the south of Chile. With its port, Talcahuano, its population is around 470,000. Like other cities in the south it has suffered repeatedly from earthquakes, the first in 1550 soon after its foundation. There is an impressive Plaza de Armas with a cathedral and municipal buildings, further out a modern university, and good beaches and seafood restaurants. Its industries include coal mining, steel, textiles and petrochemicals.

Itata SA, Agrícola y Vitivinícola

This project was initiated by the research and development organization FUNDACION CHILE (see pages 79–80), which in 1990 bought 300 hectares of land at the confluence of the Itata and Ñuble rivers, about 40 kilometres (25 miles) from the Pacific and 400 kilometres (249 miles) south of Santiago.

This is an area in the foothills of the Cordillera de la Costa where the Spaniards first planted vineyards, but where viticulture is now on the wane. By the end of 1993, 140 hectares were planted with Chardonnay, Sauvignon Blanc, Cabernet Sauvignon, Cabernet Franc, Merlot and Syrah. The vines were carefully selected from the best in Chile, France and the USA, and are drip irrigated. Leading oenologists, such as Aurelio Montes, are acting as consultants, and a state-of-the-art winery is currently under construction at a cost of US$6 million. The object of the exercise is to demonstrate that, given proper conditions, the area can support noble vines and produce fine wines. Once this has been achieved, the vineyards and winery will be sold to the private sector and the capital reinvested in further projects.

Los Angeles

This agricultural centre, with 106,000 inhabitants, lies 517 kilometres (321 miles) from Santiago on the Pan American Highway and is located in the most southerly of the wine-growing areas. A pleasant town on the fringe of the Chilean lake district, there is good skiing in season on the Antuco volcano.

Lota

Eight kilometres (5 miles) south of Concepción and beyond the mining town of Lota, where every other large building bears the name of past generations of the Cousiño family, is the famous Parque Cousiño. High above the jetties of the coal company which long ago funded COUSIÑO MACUL, the tropical gardens with their brilliant flowers, lakes and exotic birds, and glimpses of a vivid blue sea between the trees, are one of the most gorgeous sights in Chile.

Mulchén

At the southern tip of the region, VIÑA CONCHA Y TORO has a far flung outpost where Riesling and other white grapes are being grown.

Ñuble

Subregion lying west of Chillán in the foothills of the Cordillera de la Costa.

Ñuble, Cooperativa Agrícola y Vitivinícola de DO w dr r

The cooperative, serving the Ñuble area, draws on grapes of which 97 percent are grown on unirrigated land in the foothills of the Cordillera de la Costa. The great bulk of the crop is red País, but a little Sémillon/Sauvignon and Moscatel is also grown. Less than a third of the cooperative's capacity of 12.5 million litres has been utilized in recent years, and bulk wine has been bought in to meet requirements for bottled wine — 40 percent white and 60 percent red.

Quillón

Subregion southwest of Chillán in the Itata Valley.

Quillón, Cooperativa Agrícola y Vitivinícola de DO w dr sw r g

This cooperative lies off the main road from Chillán to Concepción at the centre of some 40,000 hectares of vineyards which were first planted by Spanish colonists in 1580. Of the land farmed by its members, 96 percent is unirrigated, but the cooperative differs from the others in growing rather more white grapes than red. Of these the largest proportion is Moscatel.

The cooperative is best known for its Moscatels, made with 100 percent Moscatel de Alejandría. Apart from two table wines, one aged in oak, there is a fortified 'Moscatel Dorado' dessert wine. The best of the reds is a young and very inexpensive 100 percent País, clean and fruity with a hint of blackberries.

Yumbel

The southernmost of the subregions, southeast of Concepción on the verges of the Cordillera de la Costa.

PISCO

Chile produces very little brandy in the French style, and the national spirit, made in huge quantities, is called pisco. It has been said that the name is derived from 'Piscu', which in Quechua, the language of the Incas, means 'flying bird'.

Until the late 19th century the drink was known in Chile simply as *aguardiente* or *aguardiente de vino* (grape spirit). It was first described as 'pisco' in 1871 by a producer in Vicuña in the Elqui Valley, Don Juan de Dios Pérez de Arce, whose 'Pisco Pastilla' won a gold medal at the great Paris exhibition in 1889. Before then the name had been used in Peru to describe Chilean *aguardientes*, bottled or of good quality, which were imported in large amounts through the Peruvian port of Pisco south of Lima. This has given rise to a widespread misconception that pisco originated in Peru. It did not; and Peruvian pisco, produced in much smaller quantities, is a blend of spirits made from molasses and grapes. Hence it tastes more of rum than of the delicate Moscatel and bitter almonds of the Chilean pisco, made 100 percent from grapes. The Chilean law promulgated in 1985 defines pisco as follows:

> This denomination is reserved for the *aguardiente* produced and bottled for the consumer in Regions III and IV, made by the distillation of genuine, potable wine, originating from the grape varieties [almost entirely different varieties of Moscatel] laid down by the *reglamento* and planted in the said regions.

HISTORY

The history of viticulture in the Norte Chico, the part of Chile lying between the Salado and Choapa rivers and embracing the whole of the Pisco Region, begins with the foundation of its capital, La Serena, in 1544 by Juan de Bohon, an aide of Pedro de Valdivia. After the sack of the city by the native Diaguita Indians and its rebuilding in 1549, vines brought from the Canary Islands via Peru were first planted in the valleys of the Copiapó and Elqui by Don Francisco de Aguirre, the Corregidor and Chief Justice of La Serena. Ten years later the region was making a variety of wines, ranging from the native *chicha* (see page 42) to more sophisticated growths for the soldiery and the celebration of Mass, which were fermented and stored in large clay *tinajas* proofed with pitch.

Even at this early stage copper from the local mines was being fabricated to make vessels for boiling and preserving fruit. By 1579, when Sir Francis Drake staged his raid and seized large quantities of wine (the first from Chile to reach England) and copper axles, La Serena and its port Coquimbo were the most important commercial centres in northern Chile. It is difficult to put a date on the first appearance of copper stills and the distillation of *aguardientes*, but given Spanish expertise reaching back to Moorish times, the local availability of large copper vessels and the army's needs in its far-flung expeditions, grape spirit was probably being made in Chile at least as early as its first manufacture in Holland and France.

Befitting its long history, pisco was the first alcoholic beverage to be protected by a Denominación de Origen, promulgated on 16 May 1931 and modified in 1936 and 1964, and defining the geographic areas in the III and IV Regions within which it may be produced. These are (see map, opposite) the departments of Copiapó, Huasco, La Serena, Elqui and the zones of Ovalle to the north of the rivers Limarí, Grande and Rapel.

Until the 1930s the smallholders sold their grapes or wine to a variety of private distilleries. Quality was extremely variable, and there was widespread dissatisfaction among the growers over their treatment by the distillers. As one

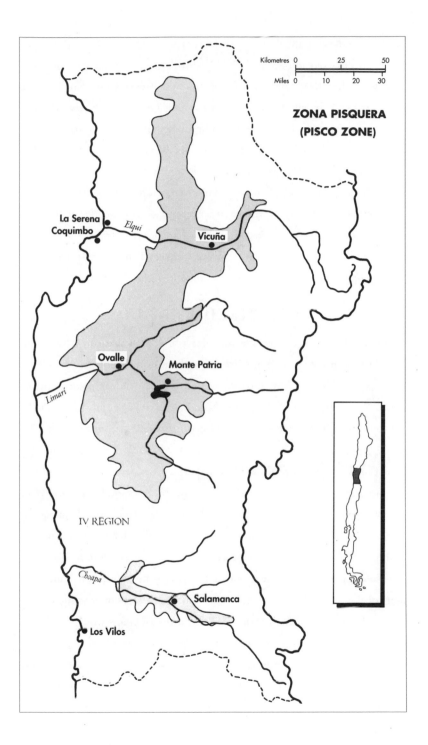

ZONA PISQUERA
(PISCO ZONE)

of the founders of the cooperative Pisco Capel, Don Ernesto Peralta of Paihuano remarked at the age of 83: 'The distilleries were trading on us. They paid what they liked, and we wended our way from one to another like drones with our baskets of fruit. It was a regular fandango. Things went well from the beginning, when we bought a house here in Paihuano for the headquarters of the Association and a distillery in the village of Diaguitas.' After the enactment of the Decree Law of 1931, the first large cooperative, Pisco Control, was formed in La Serena with modern equipment capable of making spirit of consistently high quality and with the muscle to market it countrywide. This was followed by Pisco Capel, and smaller cooperatives were set up elsewhere. Few have survived, and Control and Capel are now responsible for 95 percent of output, with a network of distilleries located across the region.

THE PISCO REGION

In his South American epic, *Nostromo*, Joseph Conrad speaks of his Golfo Placido as: 'an enormous semi-circular and unroofed temple open to the ocean, with its walls of lofty mountains hung with the mourning draperies of cloud.' Again, he describes how: 'the calm gulf is filled on most days of the year by a great body of motionless and opaque clouds . . . [until] great piles of grey and black vapours travel out slowly to seaward and vanish into thin air in the blazing heat of the day.' Internal evidence suggests that Conrad had La Serena and Coquimbo in mind when he wrote the book. Be that as it may, I know from experience that the small morning plane from Santiago to La Serena first flies above the peaks of the Andes in brilliant sunshine before, circling out to sea to make its approach, it is lost in dense cloud.

Taking the road eastwards out of La Serena into the Elqui Valley, the heart of the pisco country, the mists give way to an astounding brilliance and clarity of light, in which every detail of the arid mountains which enfold the valley and its vineyards is focussed with pinpoint precision – the terraces on the lower slopes giving way to an army of cacti and bare ochre heights roofed by an arching azure sky. It was indeed because of the luminosity and the 300 cloudless days a year that the largest astronomical observatory in the southern hemisphere was constructed on the summit of Mount Tololo, a 2,000-metre (7,000-foot) peak overlooking the valley.

The barren and at the same time fertile valleys of the Norte Chico have been inhabited from at least 4,000BC. The Molles, who first mined copper, silver and gold, were supplanted in the 6th century by the Diaguitas, best known for their remarkable polychrome pottery. They in turn were invaded by the Incas some 100 years before the Spanish invasion in 1541, so that the region is a melting pot of different cultures. Nobody has written more evocatively about the Elqui Valley than the poet and Nobel prize winner Gabriela Mistral, who was born there:

> It is a heroic slash in the mass of mountains, but so short as to be little more than a green-banked torrent, yet small as it is one comes to love it as perfect.
>
> It contains in perfection all that man could ask of a land in which to live: light, water, wine and fruit. And what fruit! The tongue which has tasted the juice of its peaches and the mouth which has eaten of its purple figs will never seek sweetness elsewhere . . .
>
> The people of Elqui take remarkable pride in their green soil . . . Wherever there is a hump, a ridge or bare patch without greenery, it is because it is naked rock. Wherever the *Elquino* has a little water and three inches of soil, however poor, he will cultivate something: peaches, vines or figs. That the leafy, polished vines climb only a little way up the mountainsides is because, if they were planted higher, they would wither in the pitiless February sun . . .

VITICULTURE

The vineyards, extending to some 6,000 hectares, are planted in the valley bottoms of the rivers flowing down from the Andes to the sea; from north to south these are the Copiapó, Huasco, Elqui, Limarí and Choapa, of which the most important are the Elqui and Limarí. The soils consist of gravels and coarse sand with alluvial deposits and are neutral or slightly alkaline. They do not readily retain water; and although the climate is tempered by cloud and sea mists near the coast, the average annual rainfall is less than 220 millimetres. With unbroken sunshine for most of the year and relative humidity of less than 60 percent, irrigation is essential in these near-desert conditions. This has traditionally been effected with a network of channels fed from the rivers, but with the high rate of evaporation and an annual rainfall deficit of 1,100 millimetres, drip irrigation is now being used successfully.

In the past the vines were planted Bordeaux fashion in *espalderas* (see page 40), known locally as the *elquino* system. This resulted in yields of 10,000–15,000 kilograms per hectare and excellent quality, and is in fact essential for the Moscatel de Alejandría, not the most vigorous of vines, for which the distilleries pay premium prices. Between 1975 and 1981 all the new plantations were of the canopied Argentinian *parronal* or pergola type affording huge yields of 25,000–40,000 kilograms per hectare and reduced quality. The present position in the Elqui Valley is that at the seaward end *parronales* predominate, giving way to *espalderas* further into the mountains.

The vine varieties authorized by the 1986 Denominación de Origen are:

Moscatel de Alejandría or	Moscatel negra
Uva Italiana	Moscatel de Austria
Moscatel blanca temprana	Chasselas musque vrai
Moscatel rosada pastilla	Muscat orange
Moscatel amarilla	Muscat de Canelli
Moscatel de Hamburg	Torontel
Moscatel de Frontignan	Pedro Jiménez

Of these, the following five varieties are the most important:

Moscatel de Alejandría

Known worldwide under some 50 different synonyms, the Moscatel de Alejandría accounts for 5 percent of production. It requires long hours of sunshine to ripen properly and in the hot climate of the Pisco Region is only moderately vigorous and cannot be grown in *parronales*. When excessively irrigated, its quality diminishes. Its wine is of high alcoholic degree, perfumed and excellent for making pisco.

Moscatel rosada

This variety, like the Moscatel de Alejandría, commands double the usual price from the distilleries, consequently two-thirds of the new vineyards have been planted with it. Apart from yielding very aromatic wines of low to medium alcoholic degree excellent for making pisco, the Moscatel rosada is grown for table grapes. Accounting for 12 percent of the vineyard area, it is not the easiest grape to cultivate, since most of the flowers are female and the larger part of the pollen is infertile, so that artificial pollenization is widely practised.

Moscatel de Austria

Introduced to the region during the last 30 years, Moscatel de Austria is easily cultivated, lending itself to *parronales*, and gives high and uniform yields. Because of this it has now been planted to the extent of some 40 percent. It makes neutral wines without marked Moscatel nose or flavour, but produces a spirit of acceptable quality, useful for blending.

Torontel

This is the Riojan Torrontés, of which it was written in its native Spain:

> *Torrontés,*
> *Ni lo comas ni lo des,*
> *Que para buen vino es.*

'Don't eat or give Torrontés, what it is good for is wine' – and it is also good for pisco. It is of high fertility, producing large yields of an aromatic wine with low acidity and medium alcoholic degree, considered of good quality for distillation. It accounts for 12 percent of the planted area.

Pedro Jiménez

This is, of course, the famous Pedro Ximénez from the sherry region. Planted to the extent of 20 percent, it has adapted well in a climate resembling that of its native Andalucía, giving large yields of a very alcoholic wine (15–16°), of good quality and especially useful for blending.

VINIFICATION AND DISTILLATION

The pisco distilleries have not undergone extensive modernization and re-equipment as have so many of the bodegas making table wines. Nevertheless there have been significant changes in the vinification so as to retain as much as possible of the fragrance of the grapes in the wine and distillate.

On arrival at the distillery, the fruit is first destalked, lightly crushed, cooled and transferred to concrete tanks, now mostly epoxy-lined, where it is macerated for four to eight hours. It is then pressed (horizontal or pneumatic-type Bucher presses are used for this), and the must is allowed to settle out before being pumped into concrete or epoxy-lined concrete fermentation tanks. In the past, fermentation took place at 28–30°C (82–86°F) and lasted for about five days. Don Fernando Herrera Enriquez, head oenologist at Pisco Control, considers that, to retain all the fragrance of the grapes, slow fermentation at 18°C (64°F) is the ideal. However, neither of the large cooperatives has sufficient capacity for this, so it now usual to ferment at about 24°C (75°F). The new wine is kept in large tanks to undergo secondary fermentation and for suspended matter to settle out, and contains 12–14 percent by volume of alcohol.

Distillation begins in early April and is carried out discontinuously at 90°C (194°F), 1,500 litres at a time, in batteries of wood-fired copper stills of the Charentais type (in the Limarí Valley, continuous stills are also used). The oldest stills with the picturesque 'swan's neck' were imported from Europe, but a modified design more suitable for making pisco has since been introduced. One feature that remains unchanged is the use of copper, which has the great advantage of combining chemically with the traces of higher fatty acids in the wine (butiric, caproic, lauric etc), which would otherwise impart a disagreeable odour to the distillate. The resulting soaps and salts are removed by regularly cleaning the still.

Only the 'heart' or middle fraction of the distillate is elaborated as pisco, the first and last fractions, the 'heads' and 'tails', being added to a fresh batch of wine and redistilled. Apart from 50–60 percent of alcohol (ethanol), the distillate contains traces of some 80 different 'impurities', these being the volatile substances which give pisco its distinctive aroma and flavour. The DO for pisco specifies that for spirit of 100 percent alcohol by volume the 'impurities' must not amount to less than 3.5 grams per litre or more than 8.0 grams per litre. Most of them are common to grape spirit and brandies in general; what are unique to pisco are the highly aromatic terpenes (linalol, geraniol, nerol etc) typical of the Moscatel grape.

After a preliminary tasting to detect any defects, the spirit is aged in large raulí or oak barrels for between four months and a year. While contributing to a smoother spirit, ageing progressively diminishes the Moscatel fragrance that makes pisco so different and so attractive, the linalol and other essential oils being converted to terpineol; it is therefore not continued beyond a year.

The spirit is then diluted – traditionally with spring water, but nowadays with purified water obtained by ion exchange – in accordance with the alcoholic degree of the final product. If the pisco is not sufficiently bright, it must be cleared with egg whites, since other agents may at the same time act as deodorants which remove the flowery fragrance.

The different grades of pisco are:

Selección	30°	Reservado	40°
Especial	35°	Gran Pisco	43°

In addition to these traditional categories, both Pisco Control and Pisco Capel are now making special piscos aged in 225-litre American oak barriques of 46° alcoholic strength.

The stronger the spirit, the longer it spends in wood, so that it is hardly surprising that the pisco with the freshest Moscatel perfume is the Selección. The higher strength spirits are intensely aromatic, but the nose tends more to bitter almonds and plums. The Gran Piscos, especially Control's new 'Gran Control de Guarda', with three months in barriques, have a very definite touch of pleasant vanilla oak.

THE PISCO INDUSTRY

When I first visited the Pisco Region, some ten years ago, the two huge cooperatives, Pisco Control and Pisco Capel, were responsible for 70 percent of production. Today their share has increased to 95 percent and many of the smaller concerns have disappeared, their plants in some cases having been taken over by Control or Capel.

PISCO CONTROL

The Cooperativa Agrícola Control de Elqui Ltda, to give it its full name, dates from 1931, shortly after the enactment of the law which established a Denominación de Origen for pisco. It was founded during the depression of the 1930s with the dual aim of establishing high standards for the production of pisco – hence the name – and making available modern technology to a host of small producers.

Its headquarters and bottling plant are located in La Serena, the historic capital of the Norte Chico de Chile (see pages 140–2) at the mouth of the River Elqui. In spite of the tourist developments and high-rise apartment blocks along the coast on its outskirts, it remains a pleasant old town with a cathedral and many colonial-style buildings and gardens, together with a most impressive railway station, alas no longer served by trains and now converted into a restaurant.

The Hotel Francisco de Aguirre, named after the first governor of the city, is the best in this part of Chile. Only a stone's throw from Control's headquarters there is an excellent market, where you can buy anything from shellfish, spices and flowers to the best and most reasonably priced Panama hats I have ever come across.

The cooperative numbers some 700 members and apart from the plant in La Serena and a distillery in Vicuña in the Elqui Valley, Control operates further plants in the Limarí Valley at Huamalata, Sotaquí, Rapel, Tulahuén and Monte Patria, and another at Salamanca in the Choapa Valley.

Its labels comprise: 'Pisco Control' in the four different categories of Selección (or Tradicional), Especial, Reservado and Gran Pisco; 'Gran Control de Guarda', matured in American oak barriques and of 36° and 46° alcoholic strength; 'Pisco Sotaquí' Tradicional of 30°; 'Gran Pisco RRR' of 43°; 'Control Sour', a bottled Pisco Sour (see page 151) made from pisco, fresh lemon juice and sugar; and 'Campanario', a cherry liqueur. The recipe for the last of these, as the label tells us, dates back to the days of Francis Drake and the other corsairs who so regularly raided La Serena. Apart from ringing the church bells to warn the townspeople of an impending raid, the redoubtable Fray Gutierrez prepared an elixir: 'to restore their lost courage and inspirit them to return to their sacked dwellings.'

PISCO CAPEL

The Cooperativa Agrícola Pisquera de Elqui Ltda, or Pisco Capel in short, was formed in 1942 as an association of some 30 smallholders who were dissatisfied with their treatment at the hands of the private distilleries. In 1964 it became a cooperative and it has now outstripped even Pisco Control in size, with some 1,300 members and distilleries across the region at Copiapó, Atacama, Vallenar (Alto del Carmen), Vicuña, Montegrande, Cerón, Sotaquí, Ovalle and Salamanca.

The headquarters and largest distillery and bottling plant are on the outskirts of the old town of Vicuña, in a hollow of the surrounding mountains. Interesting features are the Gabriela Mistral Museum, built entirely with stones from the River Elqui, and a tall wooden tower painted terracotta with imitation bricks. Now a national monument, it was erected by a Bavarian named Bauer, who arrived to install electric power in the valley and stayed on to become mayor of Vicuña. The Hostería de Vicuña, with its charming garden and terraces, is to be recommended more for Pisco Sour than for its food.

Capel's brands are: 'Pisco Capel' in the usual four grades; Pisco Especial and Gran Pisco 'Alto del Carmen', very superior and aromatic spirits from the

Huasco Valley; a ready-to-drink 'Pisco Sour En Limon'; and 'Huancara' Pajarete de Elqui, a fortified wine with a quince nose and sweet and sour pisco-like taste made from Moscatel.

The main exports of pisco are to Latin America, the USA and Germany, but are not high, amounting between Capel and Control to 247,300 litres in 1991. Home consumption is about 3 million litres annually.

The market share of the remaining independent producers has shrunk to as little as 5 percent. Among the casualties of recent years is the intriguingly named 'Pisco John Barnes', so called after an RAF fighter pilot who settled in the Norte Chico after the Second World War. The surviving firms are as follows:

Agroproductos Bauzá y Cía Ltda
'Pisco Bauzá', 'Pisco Rio Grande'

Agrícola Casaux Ltda
'Pisco Casaux', 'Pisco Carmen del Huasco'

Sociedad Agrícola Pisquera de Elqui Ltda
'Pisco Tres Cruces' (bottled for Martini & Rossi by its agents)

Sociedad Agroindustrial San Ramón Ltda
'Pisco San Ramón'

Pisco Tacam Ltda
A very small producer, which no longer bottles its pisco, but sells in bulk

Pisco Tres R Ltda
The marque still exists, but it is bottled by Pisco Control

Sociedad Productora Pisco Diaguitas
'Pisco Diaguitas'
The firm now belongs to Alberto Valdivieso, the well-known maker of sparkling and table wines (see pages 98–101)

Sociedad Agrícola Peralta
'Pisco Peralta'

Sociedad Pisquera del Huasco
Its *'Pisco Carmen del Huasco'* is now bottled by Agrícola Casaux Ltda (see above).

DRINKING PISCO

Pisco is a variety of brandy and as such may be drunk neat. It is so light and aromatic that it makes an ideal after dinner digestif, especially in summer.

Since it may contain up to 46° alcohol, we serve it in our house by pouring a little into a brandy glass and adding a couple of ice cubes.

It is also an excellent alternative to gin and vodka for making mixed drinks and cocktails, although a market survey in the USA showed that consumers used to more neutral spirits were at first disconcerted by the delicate, but definite aroma of Moscatel or burnt almonds which is its attraction to wine and brandy drinkers.

The following recipes are reproduced courtesy of Pisco Control.

PISCO SOUR

Pisco Sour, made with fresh lemon juice and ice, is drunk throughout Chile in hot weather, and indeed there are few summer drinks to touch it. The lazy man's alternatives are the bottled varieties from Pisco Control or Pisco Capel; these are agreeable enough but not surprisingly do not have the verve of the freshly made drink.

4 jiggers pisco	1 teaspoon egg white (optional)
1 jigger fresh lemon juice	sugar to taste
ice cubes	

Combine the ingredients in a cocktail shaker, shake vigorously, then strain into glasses. The egg white contributes an attractive foaming head. For a party, larger amounts may conveniently be made in a food processor or blender.

One of the most delicious I have ever been served, on a cool patio glowing with tropical flowers, was made by Doña Josette Grand, to whom I am grateful for the following recipe.

½ bottle pisco	1 egg white
1 lime or small lemon	24 ice cubes, crushed
sugar to taste	

Put all the ingredients into a food processor, blend until smooth and pour into a jug.

KIWI SOUR

3 jiggers pisco	sugar to taste
1 jigger kiwi juice	ice cubes
¼ jigger lemon juice	

Combine the ingredients in a cocktail shaker, shake vigorously and pour into small glasses. For larger quantities use a food processor or blender.

CHILEAN MANHATTAN

2 jiggers pisco	few drops Angostura bitters
1 jigger vermouth, sweet	1 maraschino cherry
or dry to taste	ice cubes

Stir the ingredients well with the ice cubes, strain into a cocktail glass and decorate with the cherry.

PISCO COLLINS

2 jiggers pisco	mineral water
1 jigger lemon juice	ice cubes
1 coffee spoon sugar	

Pour the ingredients into a tall glass, add the ice cubes, top up with soda and stir well.

PISCO ORANGE

2 jiggers pisco	sugar to taste
1 jigger fresh orange juice	ice cubes
2 jiggers dry white wine	

Combine all the ingredients and stir well, with plenty of ice cubes.

CHILEAN FOOD
by MAITE MANJON

Like most things in Chile, the cooking results from an alliance of the New World and the Old. The adaptation of Indian cooking by the Spanish invaders and the use of indigenous ingredients in their dishes gave rise to the style known as 'creole', which five centuries later is accepted as the native Chilean cuisine. However, the War of Independence and liberation from Spain opened the country up to foreign investment and development; and waves of European immigrants – British, Italian, German, and especially the French – have left their mark on the cuisine. Today, the traditional dishes are eaten at home in rural areas, but it is difficult to find them elsewhere, except in the *picadas* or city restaurants specializing in creole cooking. Only the ever-popular *empanada* (see recipe, page 170) is served without fail on Sundays in the houses of rich and poor alike.

The original inhabitants of Chile, the so-called 'changos', lived on fish from the Pacific, which in its great variety has been a major part of the diet ever since. Their successors, the Mapuches, who populated Central Chile at the time of the Spanish invasion, were people of the soil and their cooking revolved around the products of their agriculture: maize (*choclo*), potatoes (*papas*) and beans (*porotos*). Maize was the first favourite, and typical of their cooking were *humitas* (still popular today), made from stone-ground maize, flavoured with basil or sweetened, then wrapped in corn husks and boiled. Food was often cooked over heated stones. *Curanto*, for example, was prepared on Chiloe Island by layering different fish and shellfish, together with potatoes, between leaves, before cooking for an hour or so. This method was not as primitive as it might seem; the stone was volcanic and dense, thus holding the heat. The whole process much resembled cooking on a *parrilla* or barbecue, with the added advantage that the gentle heat and eventual release of steam between the layers softened the shellfish.

With an assiduous *yanacona*, or Indian maidservant, at her elbow, the Spanish housewife soon learned how to make use of the new native ingredients, and a happy example of the fusion of Mapuche and Spanish cooking is *pastel de maíz*, a pie made with minced meat and topped with sweetcorn. Meat was not, in fact, plentiful in the time of the Indians and early colonists, although *Larousse Gastronomique* describes *charquicán*, a stew made with vegetables and *charqui*, or dried meat, as the Chilean national dish. Since in the early days livestock was so scarce in the south of the country, the dried *charqui*, shipped from Valparaíso in the north, became the staple diet of the Spanish garrisons in outposts such as the naval base of Valdivieso.

Together with vegetables, fruit trees, vines and cattle, the Spaniards introduced a whole gamut of dishes, such as their rich *cazuelas* or stews (Don Quixote's beloved *olla* emerging as *cazuela a la chilena*), and such favourites as *empanadas, tortilla, paella, riñones al Jerez*, and sweets such as *pestiños, hojaldres* and *buñuelos* (later known as *picarones*). The 16th- and 17th-century wars with the Araucanian Indians had a strange culinary repercussion in that so many young men were drafted to the south that hundreds of young women despaired of finding husbands and flocked to the convents of Santiago. Here, like their counterparts in Spain, they spent much of their time making *pastelería* or sweetmeats, based on recipes handed down from the Moors. Many are still very popular today, including *manjar blanco, mantecados, polvorones, torta de huevo mole* and *dulce de membrillo* (see the glossary of Chilean Dishes, pages 163–5, for further details).

For three centuries, until the advent of the Republic in 1817, the copious creole cooking prevailed, virtually unchanged. After all, as Hernán Eyzaguirre Lyon puts it in his *Sabor y saber de la cocina chilena*: 'Without theatres or other entertainments, isolated geographically at the ends of the world, the colonists embraced the old Spanish adage: "the day is for eating and the night for sleeping".'

That most knowledgeable historian of Santiago, Benjamín Vicuña Mackenna, has drawn a vivid picture of the daily round and its climax, the great midday meal:

> The most serious act of the day for the colonists was *la comida*, served between 1pm and 2pm. The first step was to close the stout outside door to exclude visitors [at that time the wall facing the street was blank except for the door, all the windows giving on to interior patios]. After a brief prayer, came an impressive series of dishes. It began with a *cazuela* (casserole), followed by a *puchero* (stew), quickly to be reinforced by *albóndigas* (meatballs) or *chanfaina* (chopped and spiced liver and onions), *charquicán* (see above), and without fail a roast and vegetable salad. The sweets were essentially Spanish, except for *huevos chimbos* [see recipe, page 173], a dish as essentially Chilean as *charquicán* . . .
>
> After *la comida*, the citizenry retired to the bedrooms to sleep a siesta — another national institution. Nobody omitted it, and foreign visitors commented on the complete emptiness of the streets at that time of day.

Vice-Admiral John Byron (see page 12) has another amusing sidelight on the eating habits of 18th-century Santiaginos, in his entertaining *Narrative* of his adventures after being wrecked off Cape Horn in 1740:

> They eat everything so highly seasoned with red peppers, that those who are not used to it, upon their first mouthful would imagine their throats on fire for an hour afterwards: and it is a common custom here, though you have the greatest plenty at your own table, to have two or three Mulatto girls come in at the time you dine, bringing, in a little silver

plate, some of these high-seasoned ragouts, with a compliment from Donna such-a-one, who desires you will eat a little bit of what she has sent you; which must be done before her Mulatto's face, or it would be deemed a great affront.

The admiral, who spent some time on Chiloe Island before making his way north to Santiago with a handful of survivors from the wreck, comments on the excellent hams from those parts. Shipped from Chile to Peru, it seems that the meat had a very special flavour because the pigs fed on shellfish.

If the New World benefited from the plants and livestock brought by the Spanish settlers, the reverse is also true. The Conquistadors and their descendants brought back to Spain a wealth of new plants for culinary purposes; and Europe's kitchens remained innocent of such present-day staples as potatoes, tomatoes, pimientos and chocolate until they were acclimatized and grown in Spain and elsewhere. Two such commodities from Chile are of particular interest. It was at one time thought that potatoes originated in Peru, but the 19th-century French botanist, Claude Gay (see also page 22) proved that this was not so and that they were native to Chile. Although first grown in Europe around Málaga by the Catholic Monarchs, Ferdinand and Isabel, they were rejected for centuries as inedible, until grown in the gardens of Versailles by the young French botanist Antoine Parmentier and popularized by Marie Antionette, who wore a sprig of the flowers as a token of her approval.

An unforeseen outcome of the War of the Spanish Succession (1702–14) was the introduction of the first strawberries from Chile. When the Spanish colonies were blockaded by Britain and her allies, the astute Louis XIV came to the rescue by despatching shiploads of French merchandise to Santiago. He also despatched a Captain Frezier, in the guise of a merchant, to spy out the Chilean coast and its defences. The activities of the gallant captain were rendered unnecessary by the Treaty of Utrecht, but, coming from Brillat-Savarin country, what he *did* discover were the wonderful strawberries from Melipilla, which he presented to the king on his return. Subsequently propagated at Versailles, they were named *fraises* in his honour. (Chilean strawberries are still of the best, but fruit and vegetables grown in contact with the soil can cause dire stomach upheavals to visitors. Be careful where you eat them.)

As noted earlier, French influence reached its height in Chile during the latter part of the 19th century, when the wealthy mine-owners and others regularly visited Paris, educated their children there, brought back French vine stocks, furniture, paintings and fabrics, designed houses, museums and railway stations in the style of La Belle Epoque and, not surprisingly, were wholly converted to the sophisticated French cuisine.

The arrival around 1870 of a number of French chefs and restaurateurs further gave impetus to the French orientation of the cuisine. Of the restaurants which they opened, the most famous was that of François (Papá) Gage in the Calle Huérfanos in Santiago, which remained a haunt of gastronomes, writers and artists until the 1920s. It was he who introduced *foie gras* to Chile, as well as dishes like kidneys *à la brochette*, barbecued chicken, and curries. He took full advantage of the splendid local fish and shellfish, serving *vol-au-vent* of oysters, sea urchins in cases of fried bread, lobster Indian style, spiced crab meat in the shell, sole *à la normande* and *corvina* (see the glossary of Foods, page 161) *Marguery*. His *bistec a la pobre* accompanied by fried onions, although French in origin, over the years became one of the most typical Chilean dishes.

Papá Gage's wine list was as long as his menu and embraced most of the Premiers Crus from Bordeaux and Burgundy, as well as the best Chilean wines. Some of the latter, like Urmeneta, Vial, Maitén, Providencia and Benitez are now only memories, while others such as Macul, Concha y Toro, Santa Rita and Santa Carolina are still among the best today. In this Papá Gage was more catholic than some of his aristocratic clients: it is said of the redoubtable Doña Isidora Cousiño that until her dying day she never served anything at the Cousiño Palace except French wines – although countenancing its cellars to be used for distributing the Cousiño Macul wines in the capital.

A further landmark in the gastronomic history of Santiago was the opening in the early 1920s of its first international hotel, the Crillon, by another distinguished French restaurateur. Georges Kuppenheim was decorated by the Chilean government for services to the hotel industry, and the Crillon, with its elegant salons and French furniture, became the meeting point for fashionable Santiago. The *Gran Carta*, with its scores of dishes, read like the *Guide Culinaire* of Escoffier and included such delicacies as *huitres à la parisienne, congre Bercy aux champignons, lobster Neuberg, caneton à l'orange, coq au vin à la dijonnaise, civet de lièvre à la flamande, cassoulet à la toulousanne, tripes à la mode de Caen* and *boeuf à la mode*.

Although the French was the overriding influence on Chilean cooking during the late 19th and early 20th centuries, it was not the only one. The German farmers who settled in the south introduced their *strudel de manzanas* (*apfelstrudel*), which is still one of the most popular sweets; the Italians introduced a range of pasta; and British tradition was for long enshrined in the tearoom at Gath & Chaves, a department store in the style of the Buenos Aires Harrods.

Today, steaks sold by weight American-style figure largely on the menus of restaurants and hotels, but for the more adventurous, the fish, particularly the shellfish, and fruit are especially attractive. Besides lobsters, prawns, shrimps, clams and oysters, abalone (*locos*), blue crab (*jaiba*) and sea urchins (*erizos*) prepared in various ways are local specialities. As a good Scot (well, at least by courtesy), I had my doubts when I first saw salmon on a Chilean menu. In fact, the fjords and the cold waters of the far south have proved ideal for salmon farming, and since Fundación Chile (see page 79) started a research project in the early 1980s, a large industry has sprung up. Some 25,000 tons of Atlantic and Pacific salmon, as well as rainbow trout, are produced annually. The quality, either fresh or smoked, is excellent.

Chile is one of the world's largest producers of fruit and vegetables, and being in the southern hemisphere is well-placed to export to the USA and Europe out of season. Fruit-processing plants can be seen every kilometre or so driving south down the Pan American Highway, and many of the wineries own orchards as large as their vineyards, growing apples, pears, plums, cherries, avocados, oranges, lemons, apricots and peaches. Tropical fruit is widely available in season and includes kiwis, lucumas, prickly pear (*tuna* – not to be confused with the fish!), guavas, mangoes, chirimoyas and papayas (see the glossary of Foods for descriptions). Papaya cannot be eaten fresh, but boiled and preserved in syrup it is a favourite dessert all year round. Strangely, amidst this cornucopia, fresh fruit juice can be obtained only with the greatest difficulty in Chile. Hotels and restaurants serve sweetened fluids from cartons, and to obtain fresh orange juice you should ask for *zumo de naranja natural*. There is but one exception to this rule: even in the humblest establishments, fresh melon juice in season (in other words, in the autumn, March) is inexpensive and entirely delicious. Mealtimes in Chile are:

Breakfast (*Desayuno*) 7.30am–10am

Nowadays most hotels offer a buffet comprising a selection of rolls, croissants, patisserie, cereals, fruit etc. Scrambled eggs and bacon are available from heated containers, and eggs and bacon may be cooked to order.

Lunch (*Almuerzo*) 1pm–3pm

This is the main meal of the day. In colonial times and until the end of the 19th century it ran to dozens of courses and vast quantities. It is now more manageable, consisting of the normal starter, main course and dessert (plus an entrée for a more elaborate meal).

Las Once 6pm

Literally, this means 'elevenses', although it corresponds to the Spanish *merienda*, an early evening snack to bridge the gap before a late dinner. The word dates from colonial times, when it was customary to take a glass of brandy in the morning. It refers not to the time of day, but to the eleven letters of '*aguardiente*'.

Dinner (*Cena*) 9pm

This resembles lunch, but is normally a lighter meal.

Finally, visitors to Chile should note that uncooked vegetables and fruit grown in contact with the ground may cause stomach upsets and diarrhoea. This applies particularly to strawberries and green salads, and it is always safer to eat fruit with a rind or skin and to peel it.

FOODS, CULINARY TERMS AND TYPICAL DISHES

This glossary is in two parts: the first, with the Chilean names of fruit, fish, meat etc and culinary terms, to help in a food market or to understand a menu and the second with brief descriptions of Chilean dishes. It is worth knowing that the Spanish and Chilean words are sometimes entirely different.

Recipes for some popular dishes follow the glossary.

FOODS AND CULINARY TERMS

a la parrilla cooked over charcoal on a grill

aceite, aceite de oliva oil, olive oil

aceitunas olives

adobo a marinade

aguitas, aguitas medicinales
Many Chileans when offered a drink will ask for an *aguita* or herbal tea, made by infusing herbs such as mint (*menta*), rosemary (*romero*), thyme (*tomillo*), camomile (*manzanilla*), rose hips (*rosa mosqueta*) or the Paraguayan *yerba mate* in boiling water.

There are also *aguitas medicinales* for medicinal purposes, such as an infusion of lime flowers for colds. Failing Imodium or Lomotil, the best thing to do if smitten by the dreaded 'Montezuma's Revenge' is to ask the chambermaid for an *aguita*. She will provide an infusion of camomile flowers,

mint and other herbs, which is soothing and generally helpful. Other remedies for this distressing complaint are rue (*ruda*) and papaya fruit or, in extreme cases, its alkaline but bitter pips.

ají chillis – known as such everywhere but in Chile itself. Chillis, especially the seeds, can irritate the skin and eyes. To prepare them, cut around the capsule with a sharp knife, take out and discard the seeds, and wash the inside under a tap.

albacora swordfish

aliño a dressing, eg for salads

almeja clam

almíbar syrup, made by boiling sugar in water

arvejas, arvejitas green peas, *petits pois*

asado criollo barbecued meat, usually lamb

bajativo brandy or liqueur

bebida soft drink

bistec beefsteak

brocheta kebab

café Chile does not produce coffee, and in all but expensive hotels and restaurants it is usual to bring hot water and Nescafé to the table. For real coffee, go to an expresso bar and ask for *café-café expresso.*

callampa mushroom

camarones prawns

camarones de río crayfish

camote sweet potato

caracoles de mar sea-snails, boiled and eaten cold as an apéritif

caqui persimmon

cecinas *charcuterie.* The different types resemble the Spanish: *jamón ahumado*, resembling *jamón serrano* or Parma ham; *chorizo*, the orange pepper sausage, eaten as an apéritif; and *longaniza*, a rather similar sausage used in cooking.

centolla southern king crab

cereza cherry

charqui dried beef, traditional since Indian times

chirimoya Chile is the world's largest producer of chirimoyas, which command the highest price of any of its fruit exports. Looking something like a large avocado, the fruit contains large seeds and has a soft, delicately flavoured pulp with a cinnamon-like taste. It is cut into thick, juicy slices and eaten fresh, and is in season in the spring (November).

choclo maize, sweetcorn. A native of Chile, very much used in Indian and creole cookery, and first taken to Europe by the Conquistadors.

cochayuyo an edible seaweed (*Durville antarctica*)

color a popular orange-coloured sauce, made by heating garlic and paprika in oil

congrio not a conger eel as in Spanish, but a long, tubular fish (*Genyteris chilensis*) much prized in Chile. The steaks are boiled or fried.

corvina another fish (*Cilus montii*) much fancied in Chile and rather resembling a grouper. It benefits from a good sauce.

chorizo see *cecinas*

chucrut, choucroute sauerkraut

costillar ribs

damasco apricot

durazno peach

entrada a starter

erizo a sea urchin, larger than any in Europe. The edible strips of yellow-orange flesh may be bought canned and are delicious when made into a mousse or as a garnish for fish dishes.

escaveche a marinade

fiambres *charcuterie*, cold cuts and sausages (see also *cecinas*)

frambuesa raspberry

frutilla strawberry. A native of Chile, this was first brought to Europe in the early 18th century (see page 156).

granada pomegranate

guayaba guava

helado ice-cream. The best are those made with fruit such as chirimoya, papaya and lucuma.

huevo egg

    a la copa soft-boiled

    duro hard-boiled

    frito fried

    revuelto scrambled

jamón ham

jaiba an ugly-looking crab (*Cancer edwardsii*), delicious when boiled and eaten with mayonnaise

kiwi The kiwi fruit originated in China and was introduced to Chile in 1974. It has done very well in the central southern part of the country and ripens from the end of March to May.

langosta lobster

langostino crawfish

lenguado sole

lima lime

loco abalone. A shellfish, familiar to Californians and Australians, which is usually boiled and eaten cold. It is also available canned.

lomo loin

lucuma round green fruit originating from South America, with sweet-smelling yellow flesh. Harvested in April and May, it is eaten fresh and is also much used for flavouring ice-cream.

macha razor clam

maní peanut

maracuyá passion fruit

mayonesa mayonnaise

membrillo quince, quince preserve

mermelada preserve, jam; usually extremely sweet and served in small pots. It does *not* refer to the bitter English marmalade.

miel de palma 'honey' made from palm sap, coconut milk and sugar, and sold in small tins

milcao a bread made with potato flour and served with *curanto* (see page 165)

níspero loquat

ostión scallop

ostra oyster

palta avocado

pan bread

pancitos muffins

panqueque crêpe, pancake

papa potato, a native of Chile first taken to Europe by the Conquistadors (see page 156)

pasa raisin

perdíz partridge

pino a filling of chopped meat, onions and often pine kernels and raisins

pisco a brandy made by distilling Moscatel wine. The national drink of Chile, especially popular at Christmas and much drunk with lemon juice and ice as Pisco Sour (see page 151).

plato de fondo a main course

porotos beans

    granado cranberry bean

    verde green bean

postre a dessert. Many sweets are of Spanish origin – for example, *buñuelos, hojaldres, pestiños, polvorones, torta de huevo mole.* The German *apfelstrudel* is also a favourite, but perhaps the pleasantest way of finishing a meal is with the iced cakes and tarts made with fresh fruit, or with fruit itself. Papayas in syrup are also very popular.

quesillo *fromage frais*

queso cheese. Most of the cheese produced in Chile is of familiar foreign types: Gruyère, Roquefort, Camembert. The best native cheese, famous since colonial times, is Chanco made from cows' milk in Lodi in the Chico Norte and also in the Maule Region of the Central Valley. The IV Region south of Santiago also makes a good local goats' cheese.

salchicha sausage

salmón salmon. Both fresh and smoked salmon are now plentiful and of good quality thanks to large-scale fish farming in the south.

sopa soup

tocino fresh or salted belly of pork. This is sometimes served fried with eggs at breakfast, but English or North American-style bacon is increasingly being served in hotels and restaurants.

trago mixed drink or cocktail

trucha trout. Like salmon, trout is also farmed and widely available.

vacuno beef

    entrecote T bone

    filete filet, tenderloin

vaina a popular mixed drink in Chile, made by mixing port or brandy with egg yolks

zapallo squash, pumpkin

CHILEAN DISHES

ajiaco soup with strips of meat, fried onions, paprika, sweet potatoes, beaten egg, parsley, salt, pepper and cumin seeds

albóndigas meatballs made with ground veal, pork and/or ham, mixed with egg, breadcrumbs, garlic and parsley

asado criollo barbecued beef and lamb kebabs

asado de vacuno con ensalada chilena roast beef with chopped onions, tomatoes, olive oil, salt and herbs

bistec a la pobre beefsteak served with fried eggs, onions, and sweet potatoes

buñuelos sweet fritters made with a yeasty dough and fried (now usually known as *picarones*)

cazuela de ave chicken broth with sweet potatoes, rice, carrots and parsley

cazuela de vacuno beef broth served with a variety of vegetables such as sweet potatoes, corn on the cob, squash, green peppers, green beans, carrots etc

centolla con mayonesa southern king crab with mayonnaise

ceviche uncooked fish marinated in lemon or lime juice, chopped onion and spices. (See recipe for *ceviche de salmón y verduras*, page 169.)

chancho en piedra a sauce made by grinding together in a mortar tomatoes, garlic, onions, olive oil, salt, pepper and spices

charquicán a vegetable stew, made since Indian times and containing dried meat (*charqui*), potatoes, squash and sweetcorn. Onions, carrots and peas are sometimes added.

chupe de mariscos shellfish stew containing, for example, abalone, crabs, sea urchins, mussels and clams, cooked in a sauce made with butter, breadcrumbs, cheese and spices. (See recipe, page 171.)

corvina margarita corvina (a grouper-like fish) covered with a sauce made from shellfish and mushrooms

curanto shellfish, chicken, beef, pork, vegetables etc layered with cabbage leaves or seaweed and baked on heated stones

empanadas small pasties of Spanish origin made with a variety of fillings, often containing chopped meat, fried onions, olives, raisins, hard-boiled eggs etc. They are obligatory on Sundays, either as a starter or main course, and may be baked in the oven or fried. (See recipe, page 170.)

hojuelas a favourite dessert of fritters made from a dough of flour and egg yolks, fried crisp and served with golden syrup

huevos chimbos one of the most traditional of Chilean sweets, resembling the Spanish *tocino de cielo* or Portuguese *toucinho do ceu*, and made from egg yolks and vanilla-flavoured syrup. (See recipe, page 173.)

humitas an Indian dish. Grated
  sweetcorn and chopped onions
  are mixed with basil and other
  herbs, then wrapped in corn
  husks, boiled and served hot.

kuchen a sweet tart of German
  origin

locro a meat stew containing sweet
  potatoes

manjar blanco intensely sweet and
  toffee-like in consistency, this is
  made by boiling condensed milk
  in the can. It is used in a variety
  of sweets, for example with
  meringues. It is wildly popular in
  Chile and may be bought
  ready-made. (See recipe for
  parfait de manjar, page 175.)

milcao Chilean potato cake

paila marinera a rich soup
  containing fish and shellfish

pastel de choclo this traditional
  creole dish is made like a very
  exotic shepherd's pie. It contains
  chopped beef, onions, raisins,
  hard-boiled eggs and spices, and
  is topped first with pieces of
  fried chicken then with a thick
  layer of ground and seasoned
  sweetcorn before being baked in
  the oven until golden brown.
  (See recipe, page 172.)

pebre better than ketchup, this
  piquant sauce made of onions,
  vinegar, olives, garlic, chilli
  and coriander is a good

partner for meat dishes. (See
  recipe, page 166.)

pestiños small cookies of
  Andalucían origin, flavoured
  with anis and coated with honey

picarón a sweet shaped like a
  doughnut made of fried
  pumpkin batter

polvorones a powdery confection,
  wrapped in a twist of paper,
  made from ground almonds
  and confectioner's sugar and
  flavoured with either anis or
  chocolate

porotos granados an appetizing
  vegetable stew of Indian origin,
  containing *porotos* (cranberry
  beans), sweetcorn, fried onions,
  paprika, garlic and spices. (See
  recipe, page 168.)

pulmai an assortment of shellfish
  steamed in the shell and cooked
  with meat or chicken, onions
  and spices

salpicón cold meat salad with
  chopped fresh vegetables

sopaipilla bread made from
  pumpkin dough. (See recipe,
  page 167.)

tomaticán a Chilean vegetable stew

torta a sandwich cake with many
  layers

tortilla an omelette
  española a thick Spanish potato
    omelette
  francesa a French omelette

RECIPES

I have adapted eight of the recipes from that very useful booklet *Chile, Una Cocina*. Others have been given to me by Chilean friends or based on recipes in old books on Chilean cooking. I must particularly mention a book pressed into my hands by Carlos Cousiño of Viña Cousiño Macul, *Lo que he comido*, written by his grandfather Julio Subercaseaux Brown. Don Julio, who lived and studied in Paris as a young man, was one of the great Chilean gastronomes of his generation and his book contains a most interesting collection of favourite recipes, both French and Chilean. The best book on Chilean cooking generally and its history is Hernán Eyzaguirre Lyon's *Sabor y saber de la cocina chilena*. Before his death a few years ago, I was fortunate enough to meet Don Hernán at El Arlequín, the restaurant which he ran with such distinction in Santiago and where he served the best of Chilean dishes.

Quantities are given in metric, imperial and US measures.

SALSA PEBRE
PEBRE SAUCE

A piquant sauce often used in Chile instead of ketchup.
Makes 225ml / 7½fl oz / 1 cup

2 red chillis, seeds removed
2 cloves garlic, peeled
6 x 15ml spoons / 6 tbsp / 6 tbsp fresh
    coriander, finely chopped
4 spring onions, finely chopped
1 x 5ml spoon / 1 tsp / 1 tsp
    dried oregano

2 x 15ml spoons / 2 tbsp / 2 tbsp
    olive oil
2 x 15ml spoons / 2 tbsp / 2 tbsp red
    wine vinegar
salt and pepper to taste

Purée the chillis and garlic in a food processor. Add all the other ingredients and blend together well, adding a little water if the sauce is too thick. Leave for three to four hours for the flavour to develop before using.

SOPAIPILLAS

These circles made from squash and flour are served as a starter with the
piquant *pebre* sauce (see page 166) or as a dessert with syrup.

Makes 20 pieces

200g / 7oz / 1 cup squash, cooked
and puréed (boil 450g / 1lb / 1lb
fresh squash to make this
amount)

125g / 5oz / 1 cup all-purpose flour

1 x 15ml spoon / 1 tbsp / 1 tbsp
baking powder

25g / 1oz / 2 tbsp margarine

pinch of salt

olive oil for frying

In a bowl mix the squash, flour, baking powder, margarine and salt. Form into
a ball without kneading. Roll the dough until 1 centimetre (½ inch) thick and
cut out round *sopaipillas* (3 centimetres / 1½ inches in diameter). Prick with a
fork. Fry in hot olive oil until golden brown and drain on kitchen paper. Serve
with *pebre* sauce or sweet syrup.

FLAN DE BERENJENAS

AUBERGINE MOUSSE

Makes 6 individual mousses

For the mousse

1kg / 2lb / 2lb aubergines, peeled and
coarsely cut up

pinch of salt and pepper

50g / 2oz / 4 tbsp melted butter

4 eggs, beaten

300ml / 10fl oz / 2 cups double cream or
crème fraîche

For the sauce

200ml / 7fl oz / 1 cup mayonnaise

2 x 15ml spoons / 2 tbsp / 2 tbsp
tomato ketchup

100g / 4oz / 4oz fromage frais

few drops Lea & Perrins sauce

salt and pepper to taste

Boil the aubergines with a pinch of salt and pepper for about 20 minutes or
until tender, drain and add the butter and eggs. Transfer to a food processor.
Blend, adding the double cream or *crème fraîche* until smooth. Butter six

soufflé moulds and distribute the mixture between them. Cover with foil to prevent a hard crust from forming and put into a roasting dish with 5 centimetres (2 inches) of boiling water.

Cook in a preheated moderate oven (180°C/350°F/Gas Mark 4) for about one hour or a little longer. Test by inserting a thin skewer; when it emerges clean the mousses are cooked. Remove from the oven and leave to cool.

To make the sauce, put all the ingredients into a food processor and blend until smooth.

Remove each mousse from its mould by sliding a knife around the edge and upturning it onto a plate with the sauce in the middle.

POROTOS GRANADOS
INDIAN VEGETABLE STEW

Serves 8

2kg / 4lb / 4lb fresh
    cranberry beans
50ml / 2fl oz / ¼ cup olive oil
500g / 1lb / 1lb squash, peeled and
    cut into small cubes
225g / 8oz / 2 cups onions, chopped
2 cloves garlic, chopped

½ x 5ml spoon / ½ tsp / ½ tsp
    paprika powder
2 ears fresh sweetcorn, kernels only
    (frozen, defrosted sweetcorn can
    be used)
5 leaves fresh basil
salt to taste

Cook the cranberry beans in a large saucepan with plenty of salted water for one hour. Meanwhile heat the olive oil in a frying pan; add the squash, onions, garlic and paprika and cook until soft. Add this mixture to the beans. Cook over a low heat for another hour or until the beans are very tender, adding some chicken or vegetable stock if necessary. Add the sweetcorn and basil. Season and continue cooking for five minutes to amalgamate the flavours. Serve hot.

CEVICHE DE SALMON Y VERDURAS
SALMON AND VEGETABLE CEVICHE

Serves 6

750g / 1½lb / 1½lb salmon, skinned,
boned and cut into small cubes
500g / 1lb / 1lb scallops, cut into cubes
225ml / 7½fl oz / 1 cup lemon juice
225ml / 7½fl oz / 1 cup lime juice
450g / 1lb / 1lb tomatoes, peeled
and diced
200g / 7oz / 7oz spring onions,
chopped
50g / 2oz / 2oz fresh green chillis,
seeds removed, finely chopped

16 green olives, stoned and sliced
100ml / 4fl oz / ½ cup olive oil
60ml / 2fl oz / ¼ cup dry white wine
2 x 15ml spoons / 2 tbsp / 2 tbsp
white vinegar
dash of Tabasco sauce
1 x 5ml spoon / 1 tsp / 1 tsp
dried oregano
1 lettuce and 2 sliced avocados for
garnishing

Place the salmon and scallops in a bowl; add the lemon and lime juice and marinate for at least six hours (to obtain the most juice from the lemons and limes, cover with boiling water and leave for about ten minutes, then rinse under the cold tap before squeezing).

In another bowl mix the rest of the ingredients apart from the lettuce and avocados and add the drained salmon and scallops. Cover and refrigerate for two to four hours. Serve on a bed of lettuce and garnish with the sliced avocados.

EMPANADAS DE HORNO
SAVOURY PASTIES

Empanadas are served everywhere on Sundays.

Makes 20

For the dough

500g / 1lb / 4 cups all-purpose flour

1 x 15ml spoon / 1 tbsp / 1 tbsp
     baking powder

½ x 5ml spoon / ½ tsp / ½ tsp salt

1 egg yolk

1 whole egg, beaten

250ml / 8fl oz / 1½ cups warm milk

225g / 8oz / 1 cup melted shortening

For the filling

2 x 15ml / 2 tbsp / 2 tbsp olive oil

1 x 5ml spoon / 1 tsp / 1 tsp
     paprika powder

4 onions, finely chopped

½ x 5ml spoon / ½ tsp / ½ tsp each
     chilli powder, oregano and cumin

salt to taste

500g / 1lb / 1lb minced beef

3 eggs, hard-boiled and sliced

40 large raisins, soaked for about
          15 minutes in boiling water

20 black olives, stoned

Prepare the dough by sifting the flour with the baking powder and salt, then adding the egg yolk, beaten egg, milk and shortening. Mix and knead to make a stiff dough; divide into 20 pieces and roll each thinly into a circle.

To make the filling, or *pino*, heat the olive oil with the paprika in a frying pan and sauté the onions for about ten minutes until soft. Add the chilli powder, oregano, cumin and salt to taste. Now stir in the meat and cook until it is well done and brown.

Make the *empanadas* by placing a large spoonful of filling on half of each circle of dough, then add egg slices, raisins and olives. Now fold the dough over the filling, wet the edge with milk, and seal with a fork. Bake in a fairly hot preheated oven at 200°C/400°F/Gas Mark 6 until cooked and lightly browned. Serve hot.

CHUPE DE MARISCOS
SHELLFISH STEW

Serves 6

1 lobster (700g / 1½ lb/ 1½ lb) or equivalent, boiled, shelled and cut up

12 large mussels, washed, scrubbed, boiled and shells removed

12 large prawns, washed, boiled and peeled

1 large crab, boiled, shelled and cut up in large chunks

225ml / 7½fl oz / 1 cup milk or a mixture of milk and the liquid from boiling the fish

100g / 4oz / 2 cups fresh breadcrumbs

125g / 4oz / 4oz hard or firm cheese, eg Gruyère or Cheddar, thinly sliced

50g / 2oz / 4 tbsp butter

2 egg yolks

salt and pepper to taste

Tabasco sauce

4 x 15ml / 4 tbsp / 4 tbsp Parmesan cheese, grated

The shellfish other than the mussels may either be bought ready boiled from the fishmonger or cooked at home. The mussels should be boiled at home and a little of the liquid can be kept to mix with the milk for the sauce.

Put the milk, and the fish stock if used, with the breadcrumbs into a saucepan and cook gently until the sauce is medium thick. Remove from the heat and stir in the cheese, butter and egg yolks, and salt, pepper and Tabasco sauce to taste, mixing well.

Place the shellfish in an ovenproof dish, cover with the cheese sauce and sprinkle with Parmesan cheese. Bake in the middle of a moderate oven (180°C/350°F/Gas Mark 4) for 10–15 minutes or until lightly browned.

PASTEL DE CHOCLO

CORN AND MEAT PIE

One of the best and most appetizing creole dishes.

Serves 6–8

50g / 2oz / 4 tbsp butter

3 ears fresh sweetcorn (about 450g /
1lb / 1lb), kernels separated and
grated, or lightly blended in a food
processor with a little of the milk
(frozen, defrosted, sweetcorn can
be used)

4 leaves fresh basil, chopped

salt and pepper to taste

100ml / 4fl oz / ½ cup milk

1½ x 15 ml spoons / 1½ tbsp /
1½ tbsp olive oil

2 onions, finely chopped

1kg / 2lb / 2lb sirloin or rump beef or
lamb, minced

½ x 5ml spoon / ½ tsp / ½ tsp ground
cumin

2 eggs, hard-boiled and sliced

100g / 4oz / ½ cup black olives, stoned

100g / 4oz / ½ cup raisins, soaked for
about 15 minutes in boiling water

6–8 pieces chicken, cooked and boned

1 x 15ml spoon / 1 tbsp / 1 tbsp sugar

Heat the butter, sweetcorn and basil in a saucepan and season with salt and pepper to taste. Now add the milk slowly, stirring constantly until the mixture thickens. Cook over a low heat for five minutes and then set aside.

Heat the olive oil in a frying pan, then add the onions and cook slowly until translucent. Add the minced beef or lamb, cook until lightly browned, season with cumin and cook for a few more minutes. Spoon the meat filling into a buttered baking dish and top with egg slices, olives and raisins. Place the pieces of chicken on top and cover with the corn mixture. Sprinkle with sugar and bake in a fairly hot oven (200°C/400°F/ Gas Mark 6) for 30–35 minutes or until golden brown.

This dish may be made successfully with the ends of a roast of beef or lamb instead of raw meat.

HUEVOS CHIMBOS

Reminiscent of the Spanish *tocino de cielo*, this is the traditional Chilean sweet with which King Fernando VII of Spain was so enamoured when sent some by the wife of one of the Chilean deputies. The king referred to it as *postre indiano*.

Serves 6

12 egg yolks	5 x 15ml spoons / 5 tbsp / 5 tbsp water
2 egg whites	1 vanilla pod
	pinch of cloves or cinnamon
For the caramel topping	50g / 2oz / 2oz split almonds
100g / 4oz / 4oz castor sugar	

Combine the egg yolks and whites in a food processor for a few minutes. Butter an ovenproof mould or soufflé dish with a capacity of about 1.25 litres/2 pints and pour the egg mixture into it. Stand the mould in a water bath (the water should come halfway up the sides of the mould) and cook in a preheated oven at moderate heat (180°C/350°F/Gas Mark 4) for 40–50 minutes. Test by inserting a thin skewer. If it comes out clean the sweet is cooked; if not, continue cooking and test again in five or ten minutes.

Now make the caramel topping by melting the sugar in the water over a gentle heat. Scrape in a little vanilla from the pod; add a pinch of powdered cloves or cinnamon, and boil steadily until golden brown.

Remove the egg *crème* from the oven and while still hot pour the caramel over it. Wait until the caramel is completely absorbed, then demould. Cool and insert the almonds upwards on top.

This sweet is usually cut into 5-centimetre (2-inch) squares. In order to do this you should demould it into a flat, rectangular dish which makes it easier to cut up and serve.

FRITOS DE CEREZAS
CHERRY FRITTERS

Serves 4

1 egg yolk

75ml / 3fl oz / ⅓ cup milk

knob of butter, melted

60g / 2oz / ½ cup all-purpose flour

1 x 15ml spoon / 1 tbsp / 1 tbsp
    icing sugar

2 egg whites, beaten until stiff

olive oil for frying

250g / 8oz / 8oz fresh cherries, stoned,
    washed and thoroughly dried

icing sugar for dusting

Prepare the batter one hour before cooking. Beat the egg yolk with the milk and butter. Sift the flour and icing sugar into another bowl; add the egg mixture and beat until smooth. Cover and leave to stand until needed, then fold the egg whites into the mixture.

Heat the oil, pick up each cherry with a skewer and dip into the batter to coat. Now drop into the oil and fry until golden. Drain on kitchen paper and dust with icing sugar. The fritters may be served with ice-cream.

DURAZNOS RELLENOS
STUFFED PEACHES

Serves 6

3 large peaches

For the filling

2 x 15ml spoons / 2 tbsp / 2 tbsp
    ground almonds

2 x 15ml spoons / 2 tbsp /
    2 tbsp sugar

1 egg yolk

few drops almond extract

6 small rounds sponge cake

Blanch and peel the peaches, remove the stones and cut in half.

In a bowl, mix the ground almonds, sugar, egg yolk and almond extract. Distribute this filling evenly between the peaches, pressing the mixture firmly into the cavity.

Place the filled peaches in a buttered ovenproof dish, then cover and bake in a preheated moderate oven (180°C/350°F/Gas Mark 4) for 20 minutes. To serve, place the stuffed peaches on the cake rounds and top with whipped cream if desired.

PARFAIT DE MANJAR

This most popular of Chilean sweets bears no resemblance to the Spanish original, which was a most unusual sweet dish, made with chicken breasts, milk, sugar, rice flour and cloves, and served *before* a meal. The Chilean *manjar blanco*, made by boiling condensed milk, is for those with a *very sweet tooth*.

For the manjar blanco
400g / 14oz / 14oz can sweet condensed milk

Make the *manjar blanco* by putting the can into a large saucepan and covering three-quarters of it with water. Boil for about three hours and leave to cool before opening.

For the parfait	4 large eggs, yolks separated
4 x 10ml spoons / 8 tsp / 8 tsp powdered gelatine	from whites
4 x 10ml spoons / 8 tsp / 8 tsp warm water	200ml / 7fl oz / 1 cup crème fraîche or double cream
	sweet biscuit crumbs for garnishing

Dissolve the gelatine in the warm water and leave to cool in the refrigerator for about 20 minutes. Then put the gelatine into a large bowl with the *manjar blanco*. Beat the egg yolks and add them to the bowl with the *crème fraîche* or cream and mix well (this can be done in a food processor). Beat the egg whites until stiff and then gently fold them into the mixture as if making a soufflé.

Have ready a deep serving dish of approximately 2 litres/3½ pints capacity cooled in the refrigerator. Empty the dessert into it. Return to the refrigerator and sprinkle with sweet biscuit crumbs before serving.

WINE LAW

The Reglamenta Ley No 18,455 of 31 July 1986 is the latest of a series of government decrees establishing a code of practice for all engaged in production and sale of wines and alcoholic beverages. Since it contains seven main sections, subdivided into 77 *artículos*, only a summary of its more important provisions is given here.

TITULO 1

This section first defines the different classes of musts, natural and fortified wines, alcohols and spirits which are covered by the regulations.

The *reglamento* forbids the use of practices and additives not expressly authorized in what follows and outlines procedures for the Ministry of Agriculture's inspectors to obtain and test samples.

Article 6 specifies the information which must be supplied to the Ministry when seeking permission to plant a new vineyard. This includes: the location and area of the vineyard, and the areas devoted to different vine varieties; whether it is a new plantation or whether vines are to be grubbed up; whether it is irrigated or unirrigated; the system of plantation and the number of plants per hectare or the distance between them.

TITULO 2

Titulo 2 deals with spirits and the different types of alcohol, eg grape spirit, fruit alcohols, alcohols derived from cereals, potatoes etc, and synthetic alcohol.

It establishes limits for impurities in the alcohol used for different drinks, such as liqueurs, whisky, gin and vodka, and lays down individually and in detail minimum strengths for the whole range of spirits, bitters and liqueurs. The strength and composition of the four different classes of pisco (see page 147) are, for example, minutely defined. The use of colourants, except those authorized, is forbidden, and the addition of volatile 'impurities' for the enhancement of nose and flavour is totally banned.

TITULO 3

Section 3 covers fermented beverages, wine, beer, cider and *chicha* in particular. Articles 22 and 23 detail approved procedures for fermentation and acceptable additives. These include: activated carbon for decolourizing; tartaric and citric acids for correcting acidity; sulphur dioxide in small, specified amounts for sterilization and killing unwanted yeasts; tannin for clarification and as a preservative; and cultured yeasts.

Among unauthorized additives are: water; sugar; must proceeding from hybrid grapes; added alcohol; sulphur dioxide in excess of 300 milligrams per litre or more than 75 milligrams per litre in free form; and in general 'any neutralizing substance, perfume or artificial flavouring, or anything else which is not a natural component of the wine.' (This last precludes the use of sorbitol, a harmless enough but unacceptable polyhydric alcohol, used some years ago to smoothen certain young red wines, which were subsequently withdrawn. It also applies to the addition of glycerine which has, on occasion, been added for the same purpose.)

TITULO 4

The fourth section applies to the manufacture of vinegars.

TITULO 5

This relates to Denominación de Origen. The previous Wine Law of 1976 enabled the Ministry of Agriculture to establish demarcated regions and Denominaciones de Origen, but at the time only three such were detailed, for:

1   Pisco;

2   *Pajarete*, a fortified wine made in the III and IV Regions;

3   *Vino asoleado*, a fortified wine made in the unirrigated area between the Mataquito and Bío Bío rivers in the south.

Demarcation of regions and subregions for the production of beverage wines was established by the Decree Laws of 1979 and 1985 (see page 26), to which the present law refers without giving further details.

Wines may not be labelled with DO if (a) they have been grown, made or bottled outside the demarcated region, or (b) they contain *materia prima* from outside a demarcated region.

TITULO 6

Titulo 6 lays down rules for the sale of alcoholic beverages, in bulk or in bottle, and domestic or imported.

In regard to labels, the terms vino (wine) or viña (winery) may be used only in describing wines made from varieties of Vitis vinifera. Labels must incorporate the following minimum information:

Name and address of the bottler

Name or nature of the contents

Alcohol content in degrees Gay-Lussac (percent alcohol by volume)

Volume of the contents (now usually 75cl)

Where a wine is labelled with the name of a varietal, it must contain not less than 85 percent of wine made from the grape in question.

Wines with DO are labelled either with name of the demarcated region (eg Rapel) or, more usually, with that of the subregion (eg Cachapoal).

TITULO 7

Disregard of any of the provisions of the law, either by producers, distributors or retailers, is punishable by fines, sequestration of merchandise or closure of the offender's premises.

FURTHER READING

Alvarado Moore, Rodrigo, *Chile, Tierra del Vino*, 2nd ed, Editores Asociados, Santiago, 1985; *Los motivos del vino* (collected articles), privately printed, 1984

Byron, John, *The Narrative of the Honourable John Byron*, London, 1768

Carola cocina, Editorial Antarctica SA, Santiago, nd

Chile, An Exporting Country for Fruit and Vegetables, International Fruit World, Basel, nd

Chile, Una Cocina, Empresas Cochrane, Santiago, nd

Dundonald, Thomas Cochrane, Tenth Earl of, *Narrative of Services in the Liberation of Chile, Peru and Brazil*, London, 1859

El valle donde los hombres transforman el sol en Pisco, Cooperativa Agrícola Pisquera de Elqui Ltda, Vicuña, nd

Eyzaguirre Lyon, Hernán, *Sabor y saber de la cocina chilena*, Editorial Andrés Bello, Santiago, 1987

Halliday, James & Johnson, Hugh, *The Art and Science of Wine*, Mitchell Beazley, London, 1992

Hernández, Alejandro & Contreras, Gonzálo, *Wine and Vineyards of Chile*, Ediciones Copygraph, Santiago, nd [1992]

Hernández, Alejandro & Pszczôlkowski, Philippo, *La viña y el vino en Chile*, Libro Congreso OIV, Santiago, 1986

Johnson, Hugh, *The World Atlas of Wine*, Mitchell Beazley, London, 1994

La sabrosa geografía de Chile, Centro Nestlé de Información al Consumidor, Santiago, nd

Lambert Ortiz, Elizabeth, *The Book of Latin American Cookery*, Robert Hale, London, 1984

Leonard, Jonathon Norton, and the Editors of Time-Life Books, *Latin American Cooking*, Time Inc, 1970

Ministerio de Agricultura, *Reglamenta Ley No. 18,455 Que Fija Normas Sobre Producción, Elaboración y Comercialización de Alcoholes Etilicos, Bebidas Alcoholicas y Vinagres*, Santiago, 31 July 1986

Ossandon Vicuña, Dominga, *Guía de Santiago*, 7th ed, Impresora Nacional, Santiago, 1983

Paz Lagarrigue, María, *Recetas de las Rengifo*, 10th ed, Editorial Zig Zag, Santiago, 1983

Pereira Salas, Eugenio, *Apuntes para la historia de la cocina chilena*, Santiago, nd

Read, Jan, *Lord Cochrane*, Plata Press, Caracas, 1977; *The New Conquistadores*, Cassell, London, 1980; *Chilean Wines* (with Hugh Johnson), Sotheby Publications, London, 1988

The South American Handbook, Trade and Travel Publications Ltd, Bath, published annually

Subercaseaux Brown, Julio, *Lo que he comido*, Santiago, 1947

Undurraga Vicuña, Francisco Ramón, *Recuerdos de ochenta años*, Santiago, nd

Ureta, Fernando & Pszczôlkowski, Philippo, *Chile, Culture of Wine*, Editorial Kactus, Santiago, nd [1993]

Vicuña Mackenna, Benjamín, *Historia de Santiago*, Santiago, nd